D0990069

REVOLVING
COLLEGE
DOORS

REVOLVING COLLEGE DOORS

THE CAUSES AND CONSEQUENCES OF DROPPING OUT, STOPPING OUT, AND TRANSFERRING

ROBERT COPE, The University of Washington,

WILLIAM HANNAH, Council for the Advancement of Small Colleges

A WILEY-INTERSCIENCE PUBLICATION

JOHN WILEY & SONS • New York • London • Sydney • Toronto

Library of Congress Cataloging in Publication Data

Cope, Robert, 1936–
   Revolving college doors.

   "A Wiley-Interscience publication."
   Bibliography: p.
   Includes index.
   1. College dropouts. I. Hannah, William,
1919–   joint author.   II. Title.
LC148.C59   378.1'69'3   75-16472
ISBN 0-471-17124-7

Printed in the United States of America   *50341*

10 9 8 7 6 5 4 3 2 1

To

Beth, David, Kathy, Linda, Samuel, and William:

our links to change

PREFACE

Because this is a book about students as well as colleges we have tried to serve the needs of both. But we have a bias. We recognize that in all things human, as in all things natural, there are zones and times of operation—those bounds within which an entity functions. The success of functioning depends on the accord between the parameters of zones. If there is friction between the person and the place, it is the person who inevitably wears away. The result, of course, is ultimately dysfunctional for both.

It is also a book about change: changed students and the need for colleges to change. By recognizing the interrelatedness of differences and change, we do not place an unsavory connotation on the term "dropout." College faculty and administrators still, however, discourage students from withdrawing from and then reentering the campus community with ease, as if such action were detrimental to their educational experience. Unfortunately, there is a lingering negative attitude toward dropping out as a sign of failure. Even stopping out and transferring are viewed with suspicion but, as our findings indicate, these are unwarranted attitudes, unnecessarily reinforced by earlier attempts to prevent dropping out from high school (witness the advertisements on television) which has been a major, if misanthropic, part of national educational policy.

Withdrawal should not be a proscriptive term, but merely descriptive. Higher education would do well to build into its philosophy greater acceptance of change, withdrawal, and even of failure, not in a pejorative sense, but in a descriptive sense. Such a concept may prove more valuable for individuals and institutions than a concept in which success is measured only by series of unending or uninterrupted experiences.

Looking at college attrition in a nonpejorative sense allows for greater depth in probing student and college differences. We find individual people and institutions learn in various ways and circumstances and at different times. These dissimilarities are important. We also synthesize existing knowledge about attrition and retention, because generalities are important too.

We decided to write this book because we see the damage done to students' expectations of themselves when they drop out feeling that they did not fulfill their potential and it was their fault, that somehow they failed, that they had a chance and blew it—or did they? We illustrate the advantages that often accrue to individuals who withdraw, temporarily or permanently. We also write about the colleges that do not recognize the extent of the problem—where this is a problem—so they can take corrective action, both for their students' benefit and for their own academic and financial health. Finally we suggest a few things that may have an impact on national policy toward college attendance and attrition, financial aid, and institutional support.

Most of our conclusions will come as a surprise to administrators, faculty, students, parents, other researchers, and state and national policy formulators: (1) the rate of dropping out is not as large as previously estimated, especially among the talented; (2) the actual reasons for withdrawal, dropping out, and stopping out are not what they seem to be; (3) the benefits, the positive outcomes, and the reasons to encourage stopping out are substantial; (4) there are enormous differences in the rates of degree completion among different types of colleges, in fact the rate of nondegree outcomes in community college programs suggests the need to rethink the purposes of community-junior colleges; (5) precollege admissions tests are of little value in detecting probable dropouts; (6) the reasons for withdrawing have changed considerably in recent years requiring new forms of adaptation for colleges; (7) colleges should consider facilitating dropping out.

Most of the material was written specifically for this book, although we occasionally draw heavily on material we prepared for research reports and not a few journal articles. Research reports seem only to draw dust in public files and journal articles are read by a few specialists; since neither research reports nor journal articles are providing the comprehensive information needed to improve post-secondary education today, we put a little extra effort into the comprehensiveness of the bibliography as a research tool and as a base for informed application.

William Hannah, drawing on five years of work with the Project on Student Development and with the Council for the Advancement of Small Colleges, is largely responsible for preparing the chapters on college differences and the process of withdrawing. Robert Cope, utilizing several research projects at large universities and studies at a number of small liberal arts colleges, is responsible for the review of research and for preparing the other chapters.

We are not alone, however. We particularly wish to acknowledge the encouragement of Arthur Chickering and JB Hefferlin who both thought the book should be written; Diane Peters' help cannot go without special mention since she contributed greatly to an earlier draft; Jerald Bachman, William Spady, Gerald Gurin, Vincent Tinto, and Alexander Astin have conducted extensive research and made incisive interpretations in their writing on student culture which also aided us greatly in our research, in our advice to colleges and in this sharing. We also acknowledge our debt to Judy Richardson, who, against great odds, made the text more readable, Larry Richardson who worked out the bibliographic entries, and Delia Roberts who ably typed the manuscript.

ROBERT COPE

WILLIAM HANNAH

Seattle, Washington
Santa Barbara, California
April 1975

CONTENTS

TABLES

FIGURES

REVOLVING

COLLEGE

DOORS

CHAPTER ONE

DIMENSIONS OF THE PROBLEM

During the 1960s more than 10 million students met the entrance requirements of over 2500 two-year and four-year colleges and entered as freshmen. Most were expecting to earn degrees. Fewer than half graduated on schedule (within two or four years) and 30 to 40 percent, or three to four million students, will never earn degrees.

In the 1970s more than 15 million men and women are entering nearly 3000 colleges and universities, and again—since completion-dropout rates, which have not changed appreciably for decades, are holding steady—it can be predicted that about half are likely to graduate on schedule and between five and six million will never earn degrees.

Degree completion rates over a "normal" four-year college career have shown a surprisingly constant picture since the first national study (in the 1930s) indicated that approximately 60 percent of the entering freshmen did not achieve a baccalaureate degree in four years (McNeely, 1938). A similar nationwide study conducted in the 1950s concluded that 40 percent of the entering freshmen *never graduate* (Iffert, 1957). More recent reviews of the literature by Summerskill (1962) and Skaling (1971), as well as reports based on national surveys by Panos and Astin (1968), by Astin (1972), and by Bayer and others (1973), reconfirm the earlier findings: about 40 percent of the entering freshmen nationwide never achieve a baccalaureate degree.

By considering only freshmen in four-year colleges, however, the recent rates of degree completion and continuous attendance look more promising than overall completion rates that include students from community-junior colleges who are far less likely to progress to baccalaureate degrees. For example, 64.7 percent of the men and 65.4 percent of the women in Panos and Astin's 1968 study had completed four years of college in four years. Fifty percent of the men and 62 percent of the women had earned baccalaureate degrees in that period of time.[1]

The rate of dropping out among community college students is apparently considerably higher than rates at four-year colleges. Although reliable date on community colleges are difficult to find—in fact, they are usually artfully buried—nationally it appears that approximately one half of community college students do not return for a second year and only about half of the remaining students go on to complete the requirements for the associate degree. After comparing the persistence rates between four-year and two-year colleges, Astin (1975) concludes that students of comparable ability had somewhat better chances of returning for a second undergraduate year if attendance was at a four-year college or university than if attendance was at a two-year college. Our estimate is that about 2 students in 10 entering community colleges stay on to complete the requirements for an associate degree and 1 in 10 go on to complete the requirements for a baccalaureate degree.

The term dropout connotes several meanings and these should be distinguished from one another. From the perspective of the specific institution, a dropout is any loss of registration and failure to complete a degree program and therefore, anyone leaving the college without a degree is a dropout. Such a simplistic definition of dropout overlooks a substantial proportion of students who simply transfer and also may include the growing number of "stopouts," those who leave their college for a temporary period. The major concern of national studies and the definition employed in the early paragraphs of this chapter is the dropout defined in terms of a permanent failure to obtain a degree from any college.[2] We comment equally, however, on what we know about the growing proportion of transferring students and the stopouts.

By emphasizing leaving college from the student's view, we wish to balance in some small measure the preponderance of research that has treated dropout behavior from the perspective of the institution (interpreting dropping out as academic failure or treating it in terms of the cost dimensions of institutional efficiency) and from the perspective of national policy—emphasizing the production of trained certifiable manpower or the forecasting of enrollments. We also try to avoid the theoretical sociological and behavioristic approaches to understanding the dropout—at least some approaches emphasizing tables of demo-

---

[1] Bayer *et al.* (1973) in a national study *including* community college students reported a four-year baccalaureate degree rate of 51 percent for women and 41 percent for men.

[2] Nonpersistence, of course, does not necessarily mean failure on the part of student or college. Many students simply terminate their enrollment when their objective is to take a few courses or they just wanted to start college without intending to finish.

graphic statistics and behavioral correlates. We focus on the experiences and perspectives of individual students who enter college with a variety of motives, abilities, and interests and who may find higher education unsuited and often insensitive to their needs and skills.

Our research tells us it is the *fit* between student and college that accounts for most of the transferring, stopping out, and dropping out. A student from a rural background attending the large, impersonal university, for example, may find certain needs are not met; indeed, the orientation of the university and the people may be a threat, and the reaction to this situation may preclude successful adaptation to any form of higher education. The same student, if attending a small, friendly, rural college, may *still* find the institution's characteristics unsatisfactory. Relationships between student and college are not as simple as either of these illustrations. A major task of this book is to illuminate the many ways person and environment are not complementary and to suggest means of enhancing the relationship. It *is* the fit that counts.

It is also clear that the harmony between student and institution varies considerably from college to college. For example, while it may have come as a surprise to Californians that an average of only 13 percent of their entering freshmen were graduating in four years from the state college they entered (see Appendix A), these figures are typical for state colleges nationally. Different types of institutions have various average graduation rates that are directly related to selectivity.[3] Less selective institutions have the highest rates of attrition, often reaching as high as 80 percent noncompletion; attrition rates are generally higher at city and state-supported institutions than at private institutions. Later we argue that self-selection into a college of one's choice is the most important factor in maintaining active enrollment; thus the lower dropout rates at private colleges is partially the result of students selecting colleges with values that are congruent with their own.

Variations in dropout rates among and between private and public institutions are substantial, ranging from 10 percent at some highly selective, private, liberal arts colleges to 80 percent at less selective state colleges (see p. 61). The greatest proportion of attrition occurs during the first two years; the greatest proportion of withdrawals is among the academically less talented.

Table 1.1 illustrates average cumulative attrition from incoming freshman classes at 28 public colleges and universities. The largest pro-

[3]The first three pages and footnotes from the first *Newman Report* (1971) are illustrated in Appendix A because they deserve the widest possible exposure and reinforce the points made here from a slightly different perspective.

TABLE 1.1   MEAN CUMULATIVE PERCENTAGE OF INCOMING FRESHMAN ATTRITION AT THE END OF EIGHT SEMESTERS FOR 28 PUBLIC COLLEGES AND UNIVERSITIES

First	Second	Third	Fourth	Fifth	Sixth	Seventh	Eighth
8.6	22.0	28.5	33.2	43.1	44.5	48.0	50.0

portion of the 28 institutions is made up of large state universities; thus the data may indicate a norm for that class of institution. By the beginning of the second semester the data reveal that nearly 10 percent of the incoming freshmen were no longer enrolled, and by the beginning of the fifth semester (the third year) about 40 percent of the students had withdrawn. It is best to view these data as gross approximations, however, as the techniques of data gathering on student attrition vary considerably from institution to institution. We learned, for instance, that an eastern state university took its enrollment count during the fifth week of the fall term by which time, as it was learned later, several hundred incoming freshmen had already departed. Other institutions base their count on freshmen enrolling for classes the first week, while other use figures based on students appearing for orientation or paying tuition.

Attrition data gathered from a sample of 12 small, private, church-related, liberal arts colleges is illustrated in Table 1.2. These data are comparable to data in Table 1.1, suggesting that the "holding power" of the large, visible, public universities and the small, invisible, private colleges are about the same. It may be significant to call attention to the fact that the college with the highest attrition rate among the 12 has recently closed its doors.

While the national and institutional rates have not changed, there has been an alteration in the primary reasons for dropping out. There are fewer academic failures and more voluntary dropouts with student dissatisfaction and general disillusionment increasingly the motivating force (Pervin, 1965; Newman, 1971).

Another facet of the withdrawal phenomenon is that the proportion

TABLE 1.2   MEAN CUMULATIVE PERCENTAGE OF INCOMING FRESHMAN ATTRITION AT THE END OF FOUR YEARS FOR 12 PRIVATE COLLEGES

First Year	Second Year	Third Year	Fourth Year
26.8	44.7	50.7	51.7

leaving most colleges is not known. The administration and faculty simply do not know how many students are leaving and do not make an inquiry because it always *seems* the dropout rate is low. The rate seems low because most students leave quietly between terms and over the summer; they do not talk with counselors, they just do not come back (Chickering and Hannah, 1969). Their places are taken by transfers to the college and returning students.

For a rough check on the proportion of students not continuing for a degree, two easy and quick calculations are available. First, compare the number in the graduating classes with the number of incoming freshmen. The implications were thought-provoking when a community college in the northwest compared the numbers of incoming freshmen (2884, 3102, and 2809 for the years 1969, 1970, and 1971, respectively) with the number of graduates (371, 476 and 579) two years later. Second, take a simple list with 100 incoming freshmen names and compare their names among the graduates in later years.

Unfortunately, most college faculty and administrators take a we-would-rather-not-know attitude toward withdrawal data, and thus the extent of the problem—if it is a problem—is not known. There is also a he-or-she-couldn't-make-the-grade attitude. First, most institutions do not recognize the large proportion who leave and then, if discovered, assume the student must be at fault. In addition to high attrition rates it also goes unrecognized that the *majority* of withdrawing students at almost every institution we examined were doing satisfactory academic work (at least C average) at the time of withdrawal. For example, in samples taken from 12 private colleges mentioned earlier, only 21 percent left under conditions of inadequate academic performance, another 17 percent were doing marginally well, but 61 percent left under conditions of satisfactory to superior academic performance. Our studies and reviews of other research reveal that many students, especially at the more selective institutions, are leaving because of dissatisfaction with the academic process, because of the social environment, and because of the desire not to get "caught up in a meaningless rat race." In fact, some studies are beginning to report that voluntary withdrawals have significantly higher grades than do students who stay on to graduate (e.g., Mehra, 1973, p. 15).

While substantial numbers of students do not finish at the institution of original matriculation, we do now wish to imply that these students are dropouts from higher education. Many simply transfer. Some make a reassessment about their goals and abilities or are required to move because conditions beyond their control have changed, such as an illness or a family financial crisis. Sometimes they follow a loved one to another institution or they just take time out to experience another life style. In one study, for instance, at a large midwestern state university, 75 percent of the students who had withdrawn were enrolled at the time of follow-up at other colleges and universities (Cope, 1969b). The reasons for transfer are legion, and as we point out later, they usually reflect positive adjustments.

But for many of those who drop out of higher education entirely and never earn degrees—the 40 to 50 percent of all freshmen—the cost is high. Leaving often involves a substantial cost to the student in lost earnings potential and immediate out-of-pocket expenses. As irrational as it may seem, two years of college does not increase lifetime earning capacity half as much as a four-year degree. In addition, many students who do not complete their intended degree programs also experience a psychological loss; they are disappointed in themselves and must face the disappointment of family and friends.

The institution loses, too. First, substantial sums of money are devoted to attracting students, particularly to liberal arts colleges. Then, there are investments of time and energy in teaching, counseling, record maintenance, housing, and other forms of effort to accommodate student growth. There are also scholarships, loans, work-study programs—everything involving monetary cost. The graduate becomes a credit, an alumnus, or alumna, a representative. The nongraduate erodes institutional capacity and credibility.

As Withey points out, in addition to the monetary advantages of college graduation, graduates have better opportunities, more job security, better working conditions, and higher job satisfaction. Moreover, they are more optimistic about their own outlook and the national economy. They belong to more organizations, assume leadership roles more frequently, are better informed about national issues, and vote more often (Withey, 1971, pp. 130–132). In short, effective higher education is a bridge to better personal status, institutional progress, and national well-being. The effectiveness of higher education can be improved if we learn more about why a large proportion of students withdraw, what happens to them, and what can be done.

CHAPTER TWO

WHY STUDENTS LEAVE COLLEGE

Our studies have revealed that most colleges know very little about why their students withdraw. Even when records are maintained, the record is subject to the practical need for statistical simplification which erases individual human experience. Where a college maintains any record at all, the reasons for withdrawal are usually summarized as financial, academic, personal, and unknown. The categories recording the largest number of checkoffs are invariably "personal" and "unknown": personal, because it is an easy catchall for everything from a father's illness, requiring the student to return home, to pregnancy; unknown, because many students leave between academic terms, over the summer, during holiday breaks, or simply move out without talking with anyone at the college. The category "financial" is an easy excuse because it is socially acceptable and masks everything from "I am afraid of pending academic failure," to actual financial crisis at home. The category "academic" covers reasons ranging from genuine academic failure to the discovery that the college does not offer a major to satisfy a developing interest in, say, anthropology. Convenient reasons are profferred to easily satisfy the college's questions and the school fails to exert the needed effort to probe more deeply. Thus the records kept at colleges are almost worthless in their present state, a great waste of time for the institution and often an inconvenience for the student who has to fill out some form.

One study of private, church-related colleges (Hannah and McCormick, 1970) compared the information obtained by the colleges on withdrawn students with the reports of the leavers themselves. This study found that the college's information was not only incomplete but often misleading as well. According to the colleges' records, academic difficulty was an important reason for withdrawal, but according to the students, this was not so. College records showed only half of those transferring than was actually occurring. College records indicated most students planned to return to the college, which was not the case according to students. The leavers' reports ranked student dissatisfaction with the college as a higher reason for withdrawal than did the colleges' reports. Finally, Hannah and McCormick (1970) reported:

> . . . rules and emphasis on religion within the climate are not recorded by the colleges [denominational] as significant variables in data received in this study. This again would point to the "frame of reference" problem. Colleges are probably reluctant to record such data; or the student, at exit, simply is not willing to express true feelings about those aspects of the institution which he knows the administrators must defend; but he is willing to express his attitudes about these after leaving (p. 43).

DROPOUT RESEARCH

Even research designed specifically to identify factors associated with withdrawal from college, while helpful, provides surprisingly meager information: findings are often contradictory and seldom illuminate the sources of difficulty for either the student or the college. A part of the problem with such research is that few studies penetrate beyond the collection of easily collected demographic data (e.g., age, sex, SAT scores, hometown). Too many of the investigations are single variable studies that assume a particular variable (such as school size or SAT scores) can be used directly to assess academic performance or the likelihood of withdrawal. These single variable investigations take an oversimplified approach to the problem. Variables may operate concurrently as moderating, suppressing, or accentuating factors relative to academic performance, withdrawal, or other variables. That is, a given variable may be directly related, inversely related, or unrelated to other variables depending on the influence of the other unmeasured factors. The usual attempt has been to look for certain basic personality characteristics that would help one arrive at a generalized concept of the "dropout personality" rather than for those types of individual orientations that might be differentially related to attrition in various types of institutional settings.

Another aspect of oversimplification is the apparent lack of differentiation between the sexes in many studies. There is at least one good reason for considering sex differences in studies of academic performance and withdrawal: college students are in a developmental stage somewhere between childhood and adulthood; while this developmental stage has certain common needs for men and women (e.g., self-definition, developing a "philosophy of life"), there are developmental tasks, motives, and values that are different for men and women. Thus variables that are related to withdrawal of women may be different from the variables related to withdrawal of men. To unseparate the sexes for the purpose of data analysis or for action programs obscures differences that *are* sex-related.

DEFINING DROPOUTS

Defining "dropouts" is another problem. Leaving college before graduating is often considered a unitary act when in reality it includes a number of distinct phenomena. For example, some students may enter college with no intention of completing the baccalaureate degree, perhaps merely to satisfy parental wishes, to marry, or to avoid employment. For some, dropping out is an expression of an original plan.

Among the students who originally plan to complete their academic program, the reasons for dropping out are often complex and overlapping. Among the nonacademic reasons may be boredom, a "sense of wasting time," moderate financial hardship, lack of motivation, psychiatric problems (perhaps aggravated by the college experience), and so on. Several factors may be involved simultaneously in withdrawal from college, therefore making neat definitions difficult, perhaps impossible.

Furthermore, quite distinct phenomena may be operating in the case of those students who leave never to return to any college, as compared to those who leave temporarily and return to the same college or those who transfer to another college. Research and reporting that lump together all of these actions and reasons under the single heading of "dropout" are likely to obscure or confuse quite distinct phenomena.

Another limitation in most research is that studies attempt to ascertain the characteristics of dropouts versus nondropouts without considering the characteristics of the institution they are leaving. This approach is inadequate. Dropping out is an interaction between an individual and an institution. The student likely to drop out of an unstructured and "progressive" liberal arts college may be very different from the dropout from a traditionalistic religious college. Data that ignore the institutional context will rarely be generalizable from institution to institution.

In addition to these problems, studies do not employ control variables, use widely different standards of measurement, select samples using various techniques, and seldom employ follow-up techniques to obtain long-term historical data.

Despite all the limitations inherent in college records and the difficulty of interpreting research, much is known about the college dropout, whatever definition is employed. Much of what is "known" must be examined with sensitivity, however, because the results of investigations are often in conflict with each other.

ACADEMIC PREPARATION

Academic readiness is the most common variable examined, and, of course, the average score on aptitude tests has usually been found to be lower for dropouts than for graduating students. Academic ability alone, however, is not useful in any practical sense for predicting who will drop out, especially from institutions with relatively homogeneous student populations. For example, Table 2.1 illustrates admissions data from two groups of students at a highly selective, midwestern state university where about half of the incoming freshmen typically graduate among the top 10 percent in their high school class. One list consists of the records of 20 students who had withdrawn from the university by the end of two years; the other list consists of the records of 20 students who were still in attendance after two years. Remember, most students are admitted solely on the basis of the information listed here: sex, high school grade point average, high school rank, Scholastic Aptitude Test (SAT) verbal and mathematical scores. Which is the list of "dropouts"?

The students who were no longer in attendance at the beginning of the third year are in List A. Among these former entering freshmen (i.e., the dropouts), 55 percent of the men and 64 percent of the women had graduated in the top 10 percent of their high school classes and their median SAT scores were men, 556 verbal and 614 mathematical and women, 534 verbal and 536 mathematical. The persisters (List B) had higher median scores: men, 578 verbal and 636 mathematical; women, 578 verbal and 570 mathematical. While such composite medians are usually different for dropouts and persisters, it is virtually impossible, nevertheless, to identify from entrance date the student who will persist. Several investigations have not even found significant differences in the academic aptitude test scores of dropouts and persisters (Fenstemacher, 1973; Nicholson, 1973; Savicki, Schumer, and Stanfield, 1970). Their results are not typical, however.

Irvine's careful five-year study of 659 men who entered the Universi-

TABLE 2.1 DROPOUTS AND PERSISTERS: WHICH IS WHICH?

	List A					List B			
			SAT					SAT	
Sex	HSGPA*	HSR†	Verbal	Math.	Sex	HSGPA*	HSR†	Verbal	Math.
M	3.5	35/390	601	630	M	3.1	108/630	466	501
F	3.3	5/27	510	490	M	3.3	31/117	511	540
M	3.6	5/100	650	583	M	3.3	37/207	536	546
M	3.0	90/480	386	460	F	3.5	65/789	630	617
M	3.7	3/94	710	732	F	2.9	45/216	517	499
F	3.9	2/561	741	630	M	3.1	118/703	490	530
F	3.1	107/580	460	413	M	3.2	50/263	507	503
M	2.9	30/109	430	510	F	3.3	6/37	515	476
M	2.9	94/418	501	547	F	3.7	6/197	760	729
F	3.8	5/501	716	660	F	3.6	34/801	784	680
M	3.2	25/111	480	463	M	2.7	18/46	461	503
M	3.3	30/89	475	528	F	3.6	6/107	680	662
F	3.2	37/207	555	521	M	3.1	103/680	493	490
M	3.0	56/319	544	570	M	3.5	46/592	680	715
F	3.5	51/680	613	605	F	3.6	3/27	690	695
M	3.7	3/103	680	710	M	4.0	1/54	720	770
F	2.8	13/24	500	416	M	3.9	3/340	766	774
M	2.9	19/93	510	570	F	2.8	31/99	501	470
M	3.7	17/418	713	760	F	3.3	60/169	490	501
M	3.1	119/631	439	503	M	3.2	51/223	564	576

*High school grade point average.
†High school rank.

ty of Georgia in 1959 *is* typical of studies relating precollege admissions data to persistence (Irvine, 1966). He found high school grade point average to be the best single predictor of persistence; it correlated .34 with graduation from the University of Georgia, thus explaining, in the parlance of the statistician, almost 12 percent of the variation. Obviously, grades are not as important to graduation as the attention given to them in the admissions process would suggest. In a study similar to Irvine's, Mehra (1973) at the University of Alberta could account for less than 10 percent of the variation, using even more variables; furthermore, he found that the high school grade point average of voluntary withdrawals was significantly higher than that of those persisting to graduation (p. 15).

The open admissions program at the City University of New York was expected to fail because of poor retention. Guaranteeing a place in the University's freshman class for every graduating senior from New York City's high schools without regard to the conventional admissions criteria was expected to lead to massive rates of dropping out, since the University was at the same time committed to maintaining standards. While the full impact of open admissions is still open to questions about deteriorating standards, we at least know the retention rate is comparable and may exceed by a slight margin the national norm for student retention over four years (Eagle, 1973; Lavin, 1974).

As long as high schools, colleges, students, and grading systems remain as variable as they are—and hopefully, will continue to be—little reliance can be placed on performance in high school as a predictor of graduation.

APTITUDE TEST SCORES

Several forms of college aptitude test scores have been given considerable attention in attrition research. The most common are the College Entrance Examination Board's SAT-math and SAT-verbal tests, the School and College Abilities Test (SCAT), and the American College Testing Program (ACT) as well as other less well-known instruments. The general finding is that dropouts usually have lower average aptitude test scores. But, as was illustrated earlier (p. 10), these differences are not useful for an applicant-to-applicant admissions decision. Even when aptitude test scores are combined with the other "best" predictor (high school grades), the results are disappointing, even if they are "statistically significant" from the researcher's point of view and classed as "important indicators of success" by the firms marketing these tests.

When statistically significant differences are reported, there is a tendency, especially by those with limited statistical training, to impute more importance to the differences than is justified. Too often practitioners in the applied social sciences do not distinguish between the *statistical significance* and the *substantive significance* of numbers. It is of course important in research to distinguish between haphazard and systematic variations in any set of data, and tests of statistical significance represent one of the bases for making such distinctions. However, given large sample sizes, virtually any difference will be found by the conventional criteria of probability to be statistically significant. We suggest that *substantive significance* is more important: the differences are of such a magnitude and the degree of overlap in the ranges of numbered data is so small that practical decisions can be based on the results. Substantive difference is, in large measure, a matter of judgment. Accordingly, as we present findings, it is not our practice to declare certain relationships "statistically significant." This does not mean that many of the relationships discussed in this book are not statistically trustworthy—they are at least that—but more important, we try to present our quantifiable findings and our interpretations of other research in ways that show the strength of the relationships involved and permit the reader to make judgments about their substantive difference. The effect of this form of reporting makes some conclusions seem less dramatic, but hopefully more realistic. [1]

The study reported by Ivey, Peterson, and Trebbe (1966) is representative of the best we can expect when statistically combining the better precollege predictors. They used high school rank (HSR), SAT scores, and personality scales to predict attrition and reported that ". . . high school rank is the most effective predictor of collegiate success and the CEEB-SAT provides a significant addition to HSR as a predictor (p. 202)." The multiple point-biserial correlation of the three variables to attrition was .539, accounting for less than 30 percent of the variation in the criterion variables (persistence or dropping out).

In similar multivariate studies, Astin (1964), Panos and Astin (1967), Bayer (1968), and Mehra (1973) investigated the combined capability of from 36 to 120 student input variables to predict withdrawal. These studies found that the multiple correlations of all significant variables accounted for about 10 percent of the criterion variance. Time and again studies of the dropout conclude with statements similar to Bayer's: "The results of this study again illustrate our inability to predict with any great deal of accuracy which students will drop out of college and which will not" (p. 315). Yet the studies continue.

SEX

Since the precollege indicators customarily used by admissions offices (high school grade point average, rank in class, and aptitude test scores) are of little use in predicting, not to mention understanding, dropout behavior, we ask ourselves if the sex of the applicant is a possibly helpful clue to predicting. The answer is both yes and no. Yes, in that the reasons given for withdrawing are sex-related. No, when the

[1]For these observations we are indebted to R. Winch and D. Campbell (1969) for their article, "Proof? No. Evidence? Yes. The Significance of Tests of Significance," in the *American Sociologist*, **4**. 140–143, and to Jerald Bachman and his associates for their views in *Dropping Out—Problem or Symptom*, Vol. 3 in the Youth in Transaction Series, Survey Research Center, University of Michigan, 1971.

question is "Do more men or more women drop out?" While most studies report that males tend to have a higher attrition rate, some studies have found the attrition rate slightly higher for women (Astin, 1964; Holmes, 1959).

The studies of Bemis (1962), Hill (1966), Fenstemacher (1973), Iffert (1957), Knoel (1960), and Panos and Astin (1968) are typical of research attempting to determine if more men or more women drop out. Iffert's nationwide study is typical of large-scale investigations. He reported that men have a higher attrition rate (61 percent) than women (59 percent), although he did not regard this difference as significant. His study, however, was potentially biased because the Korean Conflict was taking place at the time. Knoell (1960) in her studies at California state colleges reported that more men were dismissed for academic reasons than were women; but the higher voluntary withdrawal rate of women over the four years tended to equalize the attrition rates. Hill (1966) similarly found in a study at the University of Texas that three times as many men as women were dismissed for academic reasons; but he also found that more men than women reentered after a forced withdrawal. Bemis (1962) found more men withdrawing at the University of Washington. Panos and Astin (1968) further complicate the issue by pointing out that while there was no zero-order correlation between sex and attrition, women showed a greater attrition rate when other factors (particularly high school grades) were controlled. Fenstemacher's (1973) Minnesota state college study found that "fifty-four percent of the dropouts were men and forty-six percent were women—the same proportion of men and women enrolled in the state colleges" (p. 187).

Although there is a tendency for most studies to find more men withdrawing than women, when an adequate follow-up study including reentry and transfer is conducted, little or no variation in the attrition rate for men and women is found (Cummings, 1949; Halladay and Andrew, 1958; Johnson, 1954; Panos and Astin, 1967; Pattishall and Banghart, 1957; Suddarth, 1957; Summerskill and Darling, 1955). Women tend to graduate on schedule more often than men (Astin, 1972), but men are more likely to eventually complete degree requirements (Tinto and Cullen, 1973).

REASONS GIVEN FOR WITHDRAWAL BY SEX

Even if a difference in persistence rates is confirmed, what does this mean? We are inclined to believe the *reasons* men and women give for leaving are more important. Researchers have found consistently that the reasons given for dropping out differ between the sexes (Astin,

1964; Cope, 1970; Gurin, Newcomb, and Cope, 1968; Iffert, 1957; Mehra, 1973; Panos and Astin, 1967; Slocum, 1956; Summerskill and Darling, 1955; and Summerskill, 1962).

Table 2.2 summarizes two national studies published in 1957 and 1967 that found differences in the reasons for dropping out between the sexes. The studies agreed that the major reason given for women's dropping out was marriage, whereas men tended to drop out more from dissatisfaction with college (Panos and Astin, 1967) and from lack of motivation or interest (Iffert, 1957; Panos and Astin, 1967). Finances were cited as an equally important matter for both sexes. Men more consistently than women attributed their dropping out to low grades. Frequently cited by both men and women in the more recent study was dissatisfaction with the college environment, lack of interest in studies, uncertain career plans, and uncertain major. These studies and others (Astin, 1975; Bayer, 1968; Lins and Abell, 1966; Mehra, 1973; Suczek and Alfert, 1966) illustrate that men and women consistently give dif-

TABLE 2.2   REASON GIVEN FOR DROPPING OUT BY SEX: TWO NATIONAL STUDIES

Rank of Order Mention	Men		Women	
	Iffert (1957)	Panos-Astin (1967)	Iffert (1957)	Panos-Astin (1967)
1	lack of interest in studies	dissatisfied with college environment	marriage	marriage
2	military enlistment	need time to reconsider goals, interests	took full-time job	dissatisfied with college environment
3	financial (self)	financial	financial (self)	changed career plans
4	low grades	changed career plans	lack of interest in studies	financial
5	financial (family)	low grades	financial (family)	need time to reconsider goals, interests
6	studies too difficult	marriage	low grades	pregnancy
7	military (drafted)	scholarship terminated	studies too difficult	tired of being a student

ferent reasons for withdrawal, men tending to cite internal and academic reasons while women more frequently mentioned external and nonacademic ones.

Men and women, as reported by Gurin, Newcomb, and Cope (1968), who discontinue their studies are similar when "objective" characteristics are considered, such as indices of academic competence or family backgrounds. When some of the attitudinal and value correlates associated with masculine and feminine roles in our society are considered, however, consistent differences are found. Thus intellectual-aesthetic and social orientations, which are more central to the feminine role, tend to be related to attrition for women but not for men. Feelings of adequacy and competence, more central to the masculine role, are related to attrition for men but not women:

In the data analyses the relationships of individual characteristics to attrition were examined separately for men and women respondents, on the assumption that the different needs and role expectations for men and women would make different issues relevant for attrition in the two groups. The findings indicate that some factors were related to attrition in similar ways for both men and women, but a number of differences also appeared. In general, men and women showed similar relationships to attrition when "objective" characteristics were considered—both background characteristics and indices of academic competence. Thus, for both men and women, dropping out was related to "noncosmopolitan" background characteristics such as rural and small town background and less parental education; it was also related to lower scores of indices of academic preparation (SAT scores and high school rank).

Men and women tended to differ, however, when some of the attitudinal and value correlates of these background characteristics and indices of academic competence were examined. These differences, in general, are consistent with the differential relevance of certain attitudes and values to the cultural definitions of the masculine and feminine roles in our society. Thus, intellectual-aestheic and social orientations, which are more central to the feminine role, were related to attrition for the women students but not for the men (women higher in both of these orientations tended to remain within the university). Feelings of adequacy and competence, more central to the masculine role, were related to attrition for the men but not for the women (men students with more self-questioning about their adequacy and competence more often dropped out of the university). "Identity-searching" concerns, which may reflect some sense of inadequacy in a man, were related to dropping out among the men students but to remaining in the university among the women (Gurin, et al., 1968, p. 2).

FINANCING COLLEGE.

The data in Table 2.2 indicate that the cost of financing college was a major factor in attrition, ranking relatively high among the reasons given for dropping out. The matter of money for college has been a major concern of a substantial number of studies, mostly those looking at various indices of socioeconomic status. These studies frequently report a negative correlation between variables such as parents' education, occupation, and income: the lower the level of family education, the lower the occupational position, and the lower the family income, the greater chance of being among the dropouts.

In one of the typical earlier studies carried out at Washington State College (now Washington State University) on the entering class of 1951, Slocum (1956) found that the higher the educational level of the parents, the higher the student's chances for persistence and was true for both mother's and father's educational level when analyzed separately. In another early study, Lins and Pitt (1953) found father's educational level to be related to persistence at the University of Wisconsin; 93 percent of the students whose fathers graduated from college persisted through the first four semesters, whereas, only 66 percent of students whose fathers had not graduated from high school persisted through four semesters.

The Oklahoma State Regents for Higher Education (1964) found that freshmen whose parents were both college graduates persisted through the freshman year at a 13 percent higher rate than did those from families of which neither parent had a baccalaureate degree. At the University of Michigan, Gurin, Newcomb, and Cope (1968) also found the educational level of the parents to be related to persistence in college: the lower the educational level, the greater the chance of dropping out. Warriner, Foster, and Trites (1966), studying the entering freshman class in 1962 at the University of Oklahoma, also found that student attrition was related to whether their fathers and mothers had completed high school or college.

Astin (1964), in a study of National Merit Scholars, found that the entering college students who were most likely to drop out were those who came from relatively low socioeconomic backgrounds. He found that four indicators of socioeconomic level (mother's education, father's education, father's occupation, and number of peers attending college) were significantly correlated with dropping out for both sexes.

Multiinstitutional studies by H. Astin (1970) and Jaffee and Adams (1970) using several indices of social class confirmed that children of families of higher social-class standing are more likely to persist to graduation. The father's educational level was the best single measure for distinguishing between persisters and dropouts.

This discussion of social-class status started with the observations that a leading reason given for dropping out is lack of finances and, as might be expected, family income has been an important variable in many studies of attrition. The findings are, however, less than consistent. A number of studies have found family income unrelated to persistence (Astin, 1972; Eckland, 1964a; Gonyea, 1964; Jones and Dennison, 1972; Pearlman, 1962). On the other hand, Iffert (1957), Cliff (1962), Thistlethwaite (1963b), Cope (1967), Van Alstyne (1973) and Astin (1975) reported higher income is positively related to persistence.

It is difficult to reconcile these conflicting findings. If the trend had been for the recent studies to show no relationship, it would be easier to explain, since higher income today (given union gains) is less clearly associated with higher parental education and higher occupational class.

In any case, it is our tentative conclusion that financing college is not a major problem in persistence. While a substantial number of students report they withdrew or are withdrawing because of lack of money, studies with these same students show that the less-well-to-do student's chances of obtaining a degree is equal to that of the wealthier student. Lack of money is a socially acceptable reason to discontinue attending school regardless of actual financial position. Some students who drop out are probably getting less money from home than other students with comparable family incomes if the parents have less education, because we know that less educated parents are less willing to spend money on children in college (Lansing, Lorimer, and Moriguchi, 1960; Campbell and Eckerman, 1964). As Jencks and Riesman (1968) concluded, ". . . while dropping out is probably not related to parental income, it *is* related in some cases to parental parsimony" (p. 120).

Family income, occupation, and education are unified around the concept of social class. Within social classes the process of socialization means that children acquire many of the hopes, expectations, and compulsions of their parents; they also acquire verbal and auditory skills which have an effect on their ability to adjust to the academic and social demands of college. We believe that the commitment to finish college resulting from the motivational climate of the family is far more important than having enough money in accounting for the student's own efforts to solve money problems. Many of the claims of dropping out because of finances could easily be claims of dropping out because of lack of commitment. Lack of finances is more of a barrier to starting college than it is to finishing college.

In spite of our conclusion about personal commitment versus cost of education as a reason for withdrawal, private colleges in particular recognize the importance of cost. Students can easily move from a private college to the public institution in order to reduce outlay and, although such action does not represent "real" dropping out, it does hold serious implications for private higher education.

We wish to add that personal commitment may deserve more attention both in the admissions process and in research. Our impression, not backed by our hard data, is that personal commitment to either an academic or occupational goal is the single most important determinant of persistence in college. For example, Elton and Rose (1971) have reported a major difference in the persistence rate of a small sample ($N = 137$) of vocationally decided and undecided freshmen: whereas only 17 percent of the undecided freshmen persisted to graduation, 43 percent of those who professed a career commitment graduated—even though the specific commitment may have undergone one or more changes. Abel (1966) reported that the persistence rate to graduation of failing students (less than C average) was twice as high if they were certain of their goals. And Tinto and Cullen (1973) argue (without an empirical test) that ". . . the distinction between voluntary withdrawal and academic dismissal, as well as between transfer and permanent dropout, can be more effectively analyzed by taking account of the individual's commitment to the goal of college completion" (p. 76).

Dimensions of ability, the strongest indicator of persistence in college, and dimensions of social class, the second best indicator of persistence, are obviously important to individuals, colleges, and social planners, but they are followed by a number of other important considerations:

1. Is there any relationship between a student's educational goals and persistence or withdrawal?
2. Do religious beliefs have a bearing on persistence?
3. Is high school size, college size, or place of residence related to persistence?
4. Are some psychological characteristics related to withdrawal?
5. Are some institutional characteristics related to withdrawal?

IS THERE ANY RELATIONSHIP BETWEEN A STUDENT'S EDUCATIONAL GOALS AND HIS PERSISTENCE OR WITHDRAWAL?

In a study of National Merit Scholars, Thistlethwaite (1963) reported that those students who made an early decision to go on to graduate or professional school had a better chance of graduating than those who were not contemplating graduate training. Panos and Astin (1967) found that dropouts were less likely, at the time of entrance to college, to have had plans of continuing on to professional school. Rossman and Kirk (1970) reported that 92 percent of the persisters and 77 percent of the withdrawals had, at the time of entrance, planned to graduate from Berkeley.

These findings generally suggest that educational expectations at the time of entering college may be an important variable to consider when attempting to develop predictors of academic persistence. Skaling (1971) suggested, "Perhaps researchers should not attempt to go through the back door when studying abstractly related motivational variables. Why not ask entering students what their educational expectations are?" (p. 42). Tinto and Cullen (1973) give "goal commitment" a central place in a theory explaining persistence in college, and we reiterate our conclusion regarding financing college: many of the claims of dropping out because of finances could as easily be claims of dropping out because of lack of commitment.

The relation of a student's major to dropping out or remaining in college has been examined in a number of studies but the meaning of findings is unclear. Chase (1965) did not find a significant relationship between a student's major and persisting at the University of Indiana. On the other hand, Medsker and Trent (1965), in their study of high school graduates who went on to different types of colleges, reported:

Persistence was also found to be related to the major declared by the students at the point of college entrance. It was found that the highest first year attrition group (25 per cent) were the declared terminal students, most of whom were in public two-year institutions. Next in rank (22 per cent) was the group with the business major. Those with declared majors in the natural sciences showed the greatest tendency to remain in college, with only 9 per cent failing to complete the first year (p. 97).

Reed (1968) found that liberal arts students at Skidmore College dropped out at twice the rate as students in professional fields. The Bureau of University Research, Northern Illinois University (1967) reported that the College of Education had the highest graduating rate with 38 percent graduating after four years, followed by the College of Liberal Arts and Science (26 percent), and College of Business (20 percent). Fleisch and Carson (1968), in a study of the Class of 1970 at Boston University, found that after two semesters the College of Basic Studies (a two-year program) had the highest dropout rate followed by the College of Engineering and the School of Fine and Applied Arts. The Colleges that Fleisch reported to have the lowest dropout rate were the Schools of Physical Education (Sargent College) and Education.

Bisconti and H. Astin (1973) have reported on an ambitious 10 year follow-up (1961–1971) of students with scientific majors and, although there is some question about the accuracy of these data because of high non-response rates (over 50 percent), it is reported that between 80 and 90 percent of these students had earned degrees, 59 percent within four years. Unfortunately, these data are not reliable, because of the loss of contact with over half of the students in each cohort.

IS COLLEGE MAJOR RELATED TO PERSISTENCE?

Differences in persistence rates of students with different college majors only suggest that there are different goal and personality orientations among students who may choose one major over another and consequently find particular departments or schools at different institutions either satisfying or not meeting their individual social, personality, and intellectual needs. There is no consistent evidence to suggest retention rates are better in any field of study.

DO RELIGIOUS BELIEFS HAVE A BEARING ON PERSISTENCE?

Only occasionally is religion employed as a major variable in attrition studies. In a study by one of the authors (Cope, 1967), it was found that Jewish men had a much lower dropout rate than did Roman Catholic and Protestant men and that the Jewish man was more likely to persist than was the Jewish woman. Religious preferences did not seem to be related to attrition among women.

Summerskill and Darling (1955) in a comparable study at large eastern universities with high academic standards reported similar findings. They suggested the great difference in persistence rates illustrated the influence of subcultural values and styles of life on the motivational and achievement values of students who identified with the subculture. Given the cultural value placed on education in the Jewish subculture, particularly for the male, one can better understand findings that Jewish males have a very low dropout rate in relation to males of other religious preferences, and that, to a lesser extent, Jewish females have a better persistence rate than do Christian females. These differences illustrate once again the potential influence of the cultural upbringing on one's motivational and educational values. They also illustrate the possible sex differences within a particular religious orientation.

Rossman and Kirk (1970), studying first year dropouts who left the University of California, Berkeley with a passing grade point average, found among females that 38 percent of the persisters, as compared to 50 percent of the withdrawers, were either agnostic, atheist, had no formal religion, or no religious beliefs. The persisting students were generally more likely to report that their families participated in organized religious groups. The dropouts, on the other hand, reported their families as largely agnostic, atheistic, or having no formal religion or religious beliefs.

In one of our studies (Hannah, 1970c), religiously liberal students were found to leave religiously conservative institutions while the religiously conservative student tended to move from liberal, nonreligiously-oriented colleges.

In conclusion, the limited research carried out relating religious preference to persistence or withdrawal seems to indicate that religious preference is related to withdrawal behavior. It is doubtful, however, that the practice of a religious belief is directly related to persistence; it is rather the style of life and the value orientations of particular religions rather than the religion itself which affects a person's motivation, achievement aspirations, and educational goals.

IS HIGH SCHOOL SIZE, COLLEGE SIZE, OR PLACE OF RESIDENCE RELATED TO PERSISTENCE?

The size of a student's high school appears to be unrelated to persistence. It is possible to find studies indicating lower grades and higher dropout rates among students from smaller or rural high schools (Thompson, 1953; Suddarth, 1957), just as it is possible to find studies indicating school size makes no difference (Panos and Astin, 1967; Slocum, 1956) or that students from smaller high schools do better in college (Phi Delta Kappan, 1965).

Nelson (1966) found that smaller colleges have lower dropout rates than the larger institutions, while Kamens (1971) finds, in a more carefully controlled study, that there is a tendency for larger institutions to have better retention rates. Cope (1970) concluded that a "breakeven point" may exist for each college: small colleges may have more success (in terms of persistence) with graduates of small high schools; the reverse might be true of larger colleges. It may be the fit that matters.

Several studies have considered the place of residence while attending college, approaching the residence variable several ways: rural-urban; distance to college; and living at home and commuting to college. In Summerskill's (1962) review of literature and in the report by Gurin, Newcomb, and Cope (1968), it is clear that withdrawals more frequently occur among students coming from rural, small town backgrounds and from the smaller high schools.

Regarding distance to college, Iffert (1957) stated: "The weight of evidence points to the conclusion that location of a student's home in relation to college had no bearing on his chances of graduation" (p.74). On the other hand, Aiken (1964), Mehra (1973), Stordahl (1967), and Wood (1963) found greater distance from college related to higher withdrawal rates; students often gave as their reason for transferring to another college a desire to be closer to home.

Only Iffert (1957) had anything to say about the relationship between dropping out and living at home and commuting to college; he found that students residing on campus had ". . . a significantly better persistence record than had students who lived with parents, relatives, or friends" (p. 74). He also concluded that, "Although students who lived within convenient daily traveling distance of the institutions of higher education they attended had poorer average persistence records than students who lived beyond a convenient daily traveling distance, location of home was so closely related to type of institution attended that no inference of causal relationship could be made" (p. 79). Chickering (1974), while he did not indicate the effect of commuting on college attendance, did find that the impact of the college on the commuter was less than on the student living in a residence hall.

Obviously, the literature presents conflicting findings regarding residence variables. This confusion probably results from the abstractness of the variable, that is, the remoteness of the variable from the realities of the withdrawal process. For example, among the residence variables, the best indicator of dropping out seems to be rural-urban residence. Rural-urban residence may simply be a measure of a different orientation to life, a dissimilar value structure, fostered by divergent family, community, and school environments.

Thus studies relating school size, home residence, distance to college, and the like to dropping out or academic achievement permit no easy generalization. School or community size may be closely related to levels of socioeconomic status, differences in facilities, teacher salaries, class size, available curricula, and differences in communities. For instance, who can say that a large high school in an academic community is similar to a school of comparable size in the heart of a large city or that a decentralized large university with many subcultures is "larger" than a medium size college with a homogeneous population. It *is* the fit that matters. All of these studies employing different definitions of the dropout, employing divergent variables, carried out in diverse institutions and at various times, and utilizing dissimilar samples and research techniques are virtually impossible to synthesize.

ARE SOME PSYCHOLOGICAL CHARACTERISTICS RELATED TO WITHDRAWAL?

The only other variable of general interest included in studies of the student who does not finish college is that involving psychological characteristics, that, is, personality dimensions. Whereas personality studies have increasingly been used to develop a profile of the dropout student, we are inclined to suggest that the results of these investigations have shed little light on the matter, since they suffer from the same problems of sampling, measurement, and design repeatedly mentioned in this book. The results of several of the better personality studies are, nevertheless, summarized here to provide the reader with a general idea of the results of such research. Suczek and Alfert (1966) studied transfers and nontransfers, dropouts and returnees, discovering that transfers were much like stayins, showing less maturity than either the real dropouts or the returnees. They were more conservative, conventional, compliant to authority, task oriented, and ambitious. The real dropouts valued sensations, were imaginative, enjoyed fantasy, and were motivated by rebelliousness. The returnees were seen as the most mature of all groups tested. They were complex, flexible, realistic, tolerant, adventurous, imaginative, and valued intellectual and aesthetic pursuits.

Brown (1960) indicated that male dropouts differed psychologically from female dropouts with the women scoring higher on the Minnesota Counseling Inventory in characteristics of withdrawal and depression, introversion, and social isolation with the men scoring higher on need for heterosexuality and the need for change. Brown also reported the men to be less responsible and nonconforming.

Astin (1964), using the California Psychological Inventory in a study of National Merit Scholars, found dropouts to be more aloof, self-centered, impulsive, and assertive than nondropouts. In another study of students of substantial academic promise at a highly selective college of science and engineering, it was found that nearly two thirds of the withdrawing students had psychological profiles similar to those of creative people while less than one third of the graduating students had a "creative-individual" personality profile (Center for Research and Development in Higher Education, 1967).

It is possible to find studies suggesting that withdrawing students—especially those leaving in good academic standing—are on the average autonomous, mature, intellectually committed, creative men and women who are seeking a less conventional, enriched education (Keniston, 1968; Suczek and Alfert, 1966; Trent and Ruyle, 1965). At the same time it is possible to find studies suggesting that withdrawing students tend to be irresponsible, anxious, impulsive, rebellious, unstable, and unimaginative plodders (Beahan, 1966; Brown, 1960; Grace, 1957; Gurin et al., 1968; Hannah, 1971; Spady, 1970; Vaughan, 1968).

If it is possible to come up with a psychological profile of the probable dropout, the several studies employing the Omnibus Personality Inventory (OPI) should have provided that profile, for that instrument was specifically developed to measure personality dimensions closely related to college student intellectual dispositions. Figures in Table 2.3 summarize the results of five dropout studies employing selected OPI

TABLE 2.3 CORRELATES OF DROPPING OUT FROM THE OMNIBUS PERSONALITY INVENTORY

			Studies		
OPI Scale	Cope (1968)	Hannah and McCormick (1970)	Rossman and Kirk (1969)	Medsker and Trent (1968)	Hessel (ca. 1964)
Thinking introversion	−w	*	+mw	−mw	−
Theoretical orientation	−w	*	−mw	N	N
Aestheticism	−w	*	+mw	N	+
Complexity	*	+mw	+m	*	+
Autonomy	N	+w	+w	N	−
Impulse expression	+mw	+mw	+mw	N	+
Social maturity (nonauthoritarian)	−mw	N	N	−mw	N

25

scales. Because of the employment of different versions of the OPI scales and different definitions of withdrawing students, the studies are not strictly comparable; thus we merely indicate the directionality of the scale with pluses and minuses when there is a statistically significant difference between the scores of students who had persisted and those who had not. A plus (+) indicates the dropouts had a higher score than the persister and a dash (—) that the dropout had a lower score than the persister. The subscripts m and w indicate that the difference in scores related to men (m), women (w), or men and women (mw); if there is no subscript, the report did not differentiate scores for women and men. An asterisk (*) indicates no difference between dropouts and persisters, and an "N" indicates the scale was not used or the results for that scale were not reported.

One scale, Impulse Expression, is clearly (and expectedly) related to withdrawal for both men and women for each of the four studies in which the scale was used. High scores on this scale suggest a lack of impulse control that raises questions about the ability to handle the discipline necessary to pursue a college career without some interruption. The higher scores on the complexity scale for dropouts in several of the studies suggests that students who exhibit cognitive styles emphasizing critical-independent thinking with a tolerance for ambiguity are inclined to withdraw; perhaps, in a small measure, it is intellectual curiosity that leads these students to other collegiate and noncollegiate environments. While there are differences in the other scales, the results are not consistent from study to study, and even where the results tend to be consistent across studies, it should be emphasized that the differences between withdrawing students and persisters is never dramatic; often statistical differences are "significant" when only two or three percentage points separate classes of students. Even with the results of several studies with an instrument specially prepared for the study of college students, it would be less than accurate to say there is an emerging personality profile of the student who is unlikely to complete college.

As an indication of how complex measures of personality are—as are indeed all measures—consider a further analysis that was performed on a finding reported by Cope (1968c) in a study on the aestheticism scale. It was reported that women with less interest in artistic matters and activities including literature, dramatics, painting, music, and sculpture, were more likely to withdraw. It was discovered that among women from low and medium cosmopolitan backgrounds,[2] a high aes-

---

[2]Cosmopolitan background was an index constructed on the basis of parents' level of education, urban background, and size of the high school graduating class. See Gurin, Newcomb, and Cope (p. 63) for details on the Cosmopolitan Index.

thetic orientation was associated with remaining in college; among the women from a high cosmopolitan background, a high aesthetic orientation was associated with dropping out (Gurin et al., 1968). It appeared that a certain level of aesthetic-cultural interest was satisfied in the particular college's environment and that unusually high as well as unusually low orientations in this area were less satisfied and hence associated with dropping out (see Appendix C).

One point might be reemphasized with respect to the studies that have attempted to relate attrition to individual personality characteristics: the approach has tended to be at the level of very general personality functioning rather than at the level of more specific attitudes toward values. The usual attempt has been to look for certain basic personality characteristics that would help arrive at a generalized concept of the "dropout personality" rather than for those types of individual orientations that might have differential relevance for attrition in different types of institutional settings.

PSYCHOLOGICAL STRESS

In addition to trying to assess the psychological profile of the probable dropout, there have been a number of studies on "psychological stress", most of which, as would be expected, indicate that psychological stress as an emotional problem is related to withdrawal (e.g., Wright, 1973). Psychological stress is usually poorly defined, however. It can involve everything from "feeling stress before examinations" to withdrawal because of serious depression and subsequent hospitalization (e.g., Reik, 1966).

Few studies go beyond simply relating stress to withdrawal behavior in order to probe the causes of stress, assuming of course that, since this is an academic environment, the stress is related to the pressures of scholarship. This is not necessarily so, according to our analysis of the responses from a survey of students who left a large institution noted for its academic standards. We found academic pressures (academic probation, fear of academic failure, too many C's, etc.) unrelated to self-reports of emotional upset. Instead, emotional upset was associated with the social, particularly the heterosexual, aspects of the campus environment. These social concerns, among others, included disappointments in relationships with the opposite sex (greater problem for women), disillusionment about friendships, meeting students with different standards, and not being accepted by the social groups (Cope et al., 1971, p. 107).

Our data suggest psychological stress and resulting withdrawal may be a symptom of poor social relationships, or more basic problems prior to entry into college, which, of course, may be exacerbated by the social and academic pressure in this new environment, rather than the academic environment being a cause of severe psychological stress.

Studies today should focus more on psychological discouragement (e.g., Black, 1972) or a sense of being "fed up" with college (e.g., Farine, 1973) rather than on traditional studies of a student's state of mind, which suggest abnormality.

ARE SOME INSTITUTIONAL CHARACTERISTICS RELATED TO WITHDRAWAL?

While most of the studies on factors related to attrition have obviously focused on individual rather than institutional characteristics, the latter have not been completely neglected in research. Even Iffert (1957) in his classic study, for example, found striking differences in attrition rates among the various types of colleges, with dropouts occurring more frequently in technological institutions, teachers' colleges and publicly controlled institutions. There have also been occasional attempts to deal with both individual and institutional characteristics in the same study. The most systematic has been the work of Astin who has approached the issue of dropouts using a model which indicates what is added to a variable's variance by institutional characteristics after the individual input variables have been systematically considered (Astin, 1964; Panos and Astin, 1968; Astin, 1975).

Astin (1964) attempted without much success, however, to find what institutional characteristics when added to the individual input variables helped explain attrition. In an analysis of 15 college characteristics he concluded that "No significant college effects on the male student's tendency to drop out of college were found. The female student's chances of dropping out are increased if she attends a college with a relatively high proportion of men in the student body" (p. 219). Perhaps one of the reasons why this research did not show more significant results is that Astin grouped all dropouts into one category, thus masking potentially significant differences among dropouts, stopouts, and transferees.

Panos and Astin (1968), using samples of students from 246 colleges and universities, performed a similar analysis with more variables. They suggested that two distinct, though perhaps related, patterns of college characteristics were related to higher dropout rates: (1) a pattern of interpersonal relationships marked by ". . . a high level of student competitiveness and risk-taking, a good deal of informal dating, and limited opportunities for involvement with the college through familiarity with the instructors and other extracurricular activities that tend to bring the students and college together" (p. 68); and (2) "administratively" determined environmental presses characterized by the provision of little or no structure and an apparent lack of concern about individuals' progress or conduct.

As thinking about the dropout has shifted from concern with social and practical considerations to interest in integrating theoretical and practical concerns, there has been a growing interest in an interactive approach to the issue, one which views dropping out not as an individual or an institutional problem, but one involving the harmony or lack of it between the individual and the institutional environment. Two examples of such research which vary greatly in their orientations and the dimensions they study are the works of Pervin and Rubin (1967) and Keniston and Helmreich (1965). Pervin and Rubin were mainly concerned with *perceptual* congruence, relating probable drop out for nonacademic reasons to the discrepancies between a student's perception of his self and his college, his self and other students, his college and the ideal college. Keniston and Helmreich, on the other hand, structure the problem around the identity issues that have been Keniston's concern in much of his research and writings. They view the congruence or lack of congruence of a college environment with a student in terms of the promotion or thwarting of the student's identity development. Keniston and Helmreich were also interested in the personality traits that are related to a student's remaining in college even under a high degree of discordance, traits such as the tolerance of frustration, the "protestant ethic," alienation and rebellion against parents.

The congruence model has also occasionally been applied in relating attrition to different subenvironments within a given institution. The study by Nasatir (1969) represents one of the few systematic, quantitative applications of this model to a study of attrition. Nasatir characterized individuals and their dormitories according to their "academic" or "nonacademic" orientation and indicated that academic failure was greatest where there was an incongruence between the dominant orientation of the individual and that of his dormitory.

In addition to research programs and studies specifically designed around an interaction approach, the influence of this point of view can be seen increasingly in the interpretation given to results in studies of dropouts even when the research was not specifically designed around such a model. Thus Suczek and Alfert (1966), in interpreting the unexpected finding that dropouts (that is, dropouts in "good standing") were more mature, sophisticated, and less narrowly conventional than the nondropouts, suggested that these dropouts' maturity may have made them dissatisfied and uncomfortable with the petty and restrictive demands of their environment at Berkeley.

The quality of the college has also been related to persistence by Astin (1975), Kamens (1971), Wegner (1967), and Wegner and Sewell (1970). The findings generally indicate that students in the higher quality institutions—measured by average ability of students, proportion of doctorates on faculty, and expenditures per student—are more likely to graduate than are students of similar ability, with similar aspirations, attending lower quality institutions. The lowest quality institutions tend to have the lowest graduation rates for all types of students according to the results of a national study by Kamens (1971), but not according to Wegner (1967), who reported in a study involving a sample of colleges in Wisconsin, that retention rates were best for low-status and high-ability students or less able students if they attended institutions of either very high or very low quality. While it is clear all types of students are more likely to persist to graduation in higher quality institutions, the effect of attendance at lower quality institutions is less clear.

In Chapter 7 we suggest more productive procedures for action research on college attrition designed to clarify how students may be helped and, consequently, how institutions may help themselves become more creditable and more adept at maintaining higher enrollments. The references following the text have been extended well beyond those we refer to in this book as a guide to research. The next chapters, on how different students really are, and on the process of withdrawing, suggest the difficulty of both action programs and basic research.

CHAPTER THREE

DIFFERENT STUDENTS, DIFFERENT REASONS

Complex dynamics of person-institution-life style are but feebly captured by numbers that report on school leavers in frequencies, percentages, means, standard deviations, and levels of statistical significance. Quantification obscures the human dimensions, the nonqualifiables such as uncertainty and ambivalence, questing for independence, reassessments, and experiential learning. For analytic purposes the usual research also tends to isolate *quantifiable* student characteristics leading to general predispositions to drop out (those characteristics that are viewed as providing problems for any student) without providing *qualitative* insights originating with individuals in their setting. This chapter delves into the qualitative, into the realm of feeling, into the multifaceted interaction between person and setting to illuminate the problems confronting students that have not been brought out in previous research. These are the kind of problems that are not clearly discernible without going to the students themselves to obtain their candid comments. In this process we make generalizations, which, like Procrustes, lop off some height or length while stretching a point here and there.

We rely heavily on our studies of college leaving for these observations, and use the selected remarks of students for illustration. The Sues, Toms, and Pauls are clearly not representative of all students, and that is the main point: as we grasp for understanding, we must not forget the multiple combinations and varied lengths and weights that operate for individuals. The remarks are compiled from follow-up questionnaires and from interviews with students who had already left college or who subsequently withdrew. [1]

POOR CHOICE

It is readily apparent that many students leave the college of first matriculation because they simply make a poor choice. Poor choice is often *not* a matter of inadequate academic promise on their part, but is often a matter of insufficient *intellectual* challenge. For example, these comments are from three students who transferred from a prestigious midwestern public university after their first year:

I'm afraid that I found my year at the University rather dry and sterile. The problem is multidimensional but I think that the place to start is with the undergraduate student body. Generally, I found my fellow students either incapable or not interested in carrying discussions from the classroom back to the dorm.

Little intellectual activity at the University undergraduate school. Ossification of values of most students. Whole University permeated with vocational-vulgar-pragmatic attitude toward education.

I couldn't see any reason to attend the University other than the degree; there was no intellectual stimulation; most of the students had the same socioeconomic background.

These students seem to place most of the emphasis on the "intellectual climate" of the institution while other students, who likewise apparently made a similar mistake attending the same institution, seem more concerned about the lack of "cosmopolitanism;" they find the institution's *social* climate stifling:

I didn't like the Midwest. My courses weren't as stimulating as I'd hoped. The students were mostly self-satisfied, middle-class conformists with narrow minds. Generally, I wasn't happy with the people.

I missed the variety of experiences and people that New York offers; I found that a huge university in a small town offered little respite from a "school-conscious" atmosphere.

After two years, the "campus life" was a meaningless and boring one and my

[1]In addition to these interviews, we recommend two lengthy letters, included in Appendix B, that bring out the many and often complexly interrelated reasons for withdrawal.

little world a very narrow and unreal world. I wanted a city school where I would not have as much pressure to play "undergraduate co-ed" so I transferred to University of Pennsylvania.

These "intellective-cosmopolitan dropouts," which appear to average about 5 percent of most institutions' leavers, are polar opposites to the transferring students who find either the campus social climate or academic pressures (or both) too much and usually express themselves this way:

It was very different from my high school where I knew everyone. It's bigness and cold attitude was disheartening and disappointing to me, although my grades were satisfactory.

I felt lost among the multitudes, never really fitting in or finding satisfactory friendship among students or faculty. I also had difficulty concentrating on studies because of my depression. I didn't think it worthwhile to continue with this attitude and state of mind.

I was very homesick and overwhelmed by the impersonal atmosphere, as well as the diversity of characters I came in contact with. I also had no idea of how to study, thought that if I was smart enough to have been accepted, I could glide by without studying as I had done in high school. I felt as if no one cared if I flunked out or not.

A substantial proportion of students thus appear to transfer from the college of first matriculation simply because of having made a poor assessment of the social and intellectual climate.[2] Our estimate is that this is the primary reason for at least 20 percent of those who transfer. Many students simply stick with it—the "walking wounded."

It is not only that they make a poor choice of "climate"; some students are almost totally uninformed about rudimentary matters, another form of poor choice:

I wanted to go to law school and discovered the University did not have a law school. I thought all universities had law schools.

I learned during the first semester that it would not be possible to earn a teaching certificate at the college. I didn't know it was necessary to go only to certain colleges to become a teacher.

---

[2]Because the intellectual-social climate—some would call it the environmental press—illustrates what we mean by person-institution fit and also suggests the nature of the congruency mechanism operating as students self-select themselves out or are "pushed" out of colleges, we go into a little more detail in Appendix C.

BUREAUCRACY

While it seldom leads directly to withdrawal, in combination with other matters the bureaucratic atmosphere in large universities causes students to develop negative attitudes toward continuance; dealing with the bureaucracy becomes one more "cost" to consider against the benefit of the degree or of learning something. Here is part of the response from a woman who, although doing well academically, decided to leave a large university to pursue a certificate program in a local business college:

I felt it a ridiculous waste of time to have program cards signed. Standing in line to get your classrooms arranged is equally maddening only to find yourself in classes of 100–200 plus students which are too large to provide anything more than third-rate mass production on a few items too freely included under "education." Faculty was rarely available for assistance and then if I got five minutes with one I felt rushed! Basically, I resented the impersonal attitude of professors and T.A.s [teaching assistants]. Being treated like an irresponsible child seems reason enough to be disappointed with the system; i.e., if the class as a whole did poorly on a given exam, the professor would spend the next lecture period berating the students—"stupid," "dumb," etc., rather than explaining what he or she failed to get across the first time.

Another woman who had withdrawn, transferring to attend a nonaccredited school of commercial art, felt this way about her semester at a research-oriented university:

I felt like a machine programmed with absurd material. The good teachers—humane ones with time for their students—were not rewarded. Undergraduate years are viewed as something to undergo, to get through. In two classes I had T.A.s who were dismally unprepared, boring lecturers who completely failed to convey any meaning to their students. Don't T.A.s have any training? How can a university justify charging tuition for such teaching?

The problems with the bureaucracy and T.A.s appears not to be related to size per se. We find responses from leavers from some institutions almost devoid of bureaucratic-related items; these institutions apparently, despite their size, keep frustrating regulations at a minimum. Other institutions, and they can be relatively small among colleges and universities, seem to make excessive demands to fill out the proper form completely, with the right signatures, at the appointed time, and leave it with the correct office.

When sheer size is a problem, it is not a problem for only the student from a small town. Consider the young man from New York City who went west to attend a large state university in a small town:

I am back as a full time student at New York University (University Heights) . . . . I was overwhelmed by the size and impersonal atmosphere of the University and couldn't concentrate on my work . . . decided to return home to think things over.

TEACHING QUALITY

Seldom an important problem for students who leave the liberal arts college, but a significant area of concern among those (usually women) leaving the large university, are the quality of teaching, the size of classes, and the reliance on lecturing:

Most of the classes I took were disappointing and I wasn't learning anything. I felt stifled in large classrooms and in an atmosphere of competition among students instead of concentration on self-development. I wanted to learn as a part of inner development but since the University isn't oriented that way, it was useless to me.

An atmosphere conducive to the asking of questions seemed to be lacking in many of my large lecture classes. Just the sheer huge numbers turning around to look at you as you would speak was enough to scare you into silence.

Another concern of mine was the general lack of competent lecturers at the U. A student can be absolutely turned on by the course material, but after having to sit through five hours a week of a boring lecture series, the exciting quality gets drowned in a prof's monotone drone.

IDENTITY SEEKING

Erikson and others (e.g., Chickering, 1969) have perceptively viewed the college years as providing a psycho-social moratorium for testing and trying out different alternatives in the complex process of identity formation, viewed by many as one of the critical tasks of the college years. Students vary greatly, however, in the extent to which this identity-forming process is a critical and conscious concern and thus, while there is evidence that identity crises usually lead students to become stop outs and sometimes to withdraw from higher education entirely, the extent to which this is a dropout problem is difficult to assess. The person who is apparently working through a question of identity will say something about leaving "to find myself, to discover what kind of person I really want to be, to have an opportunity to think through what I really believe, to discover what values are important to me . . . ." Many of the comments heard from students about the need for relevance is really an unrecognized way of saying, "Help me discover who

I am." Such students usually drop out of college with the intent to return, often to the same institution. A woman after one quarter remarked:

> I came to college because I thought it would be a good place to explore my own potential . . . to find out if what I want to do means graduating or dropping out to find something better. I've found out that college isn't for me, and the Program [an experimental residential college] has helped me decide. Mostly by talking with the other kids, the books we did—especially Camus—and especially the chance to talk to some older people (counselors) who've been thru it all . . . .

> I want to prepare myself intellectually, emotionally, and practically to face the world on my own. I realize this sounds very vague, and that my goals are perhaps romantic and long range, but that's the best I can do right now. I also know that my learning will not stop when I drop out. In a way I think that learning only begins when you get out of the institution and on your own, having to use your ideas to live on and to amuse yourself with.

Another woman after two years commented:

> The things that concerned me most were: disillusionment with the purpose of college education, the failure of coursework to challenge me intellectually, impatience with superficiality, and a feeling that the college isn't doing enough to promote change. Today students want some relevance in their education and they have a right to demand it. At present, the college is too isolated from the real world. After four years in such an atmosphere it takes a great deal of adjusting to function in that real world in a constructive and meaningful way.

While it is obvious that uncertainty about one's identity (goals, direction in life) may bring about withdrawal to "find myself," it may be surprising that *finding* one's self is likewise a reason for withdrawal, usually for reasons we applaud:

> It took me two years to realize that what I wanted most was to return to farming and a degree from a liberal arts college no longer seems important. I enjoyed my fellow students and did well at the college but now I am shoeing horses to earn money for a down payment on a farm. This *is* the life.

> I decided to major in business administration and since the college does not offer this degree I transferred to the University.

> I grew up in a sheltered home. My mother and father decided everything, even which college to attend and my major. I was a very gullible person, always following whatever someone suggested. I guess it was because I always felt inferior and insecure. The first two years I felt sort of desperately lost and I did everything expected of me so I pulled good grades, now I know what is important and what isn't, so I am quitting school after this term.

Others *are* seeking the real world or at least so it seems:

I couldn't take the rarified theories of the Political Science Department. The professors were talking about countries they've never even been to.

After I experience a bit more of real living and finding out about real people, where they live and work, I will be able to separate the useful knowledge from the pure bullshit. For example, just now I am coming to realize how incompetent most people are—they need help—and not the kind that finds its way into textbooks. I was a business major; that means lots of accounting, finance, business law, real estate and the like, but I find the real problems are office politics and personalities. This is education.

I enjoyed the college, was getting good grades, had nice friends—I was just plain comfortable, too comfortable. It was unreal.

After the first year (at the college) I spent the summer working (my first job) in St. Louis, fully intending to return in the fall, but it was not long before I discovered how incredibly dumb and naive I was about the world and about people. Everything seemed so simple at home and at the college. Life was not as stimulating as it is now. I don't think I can return to a campus school so I am attending classes at a junior college in the evening. I may earn a degree, but it's not important anymore.

One can hardly be in the program without taking a more thoughtful look at the process of education. It wasn't easy, but it was certainly worth the effort. I'm leaving to clarify in my own mind my educational goals—to try out uninstitutionalized learning for a while.

VALUE CONFRONTATIONS

In some instances, conflicts of values among students force individuals to positions of self-doubt, defensiveness, and possible reevaluation, especially when one's values run counter to values predominating in the college environment. The areas of conflict nearly always concern religion, morality-sexuality standards, and politics, and usually occur during the first year of college.

Confrontations in religious values are probably the dominant area of confrontation among men and women equally, while women, far more often than men, are challenged by other students in the area of morality and sexual standards. Challenges to both religious and morality standards appear to result in reevaluations, sometime painful, and when combined with other stresses lead to withdrawal. Challenges to political beliefs (usually conservative-liberal), however, do not appear to have an effect on withdrawal.

The psychic stresses and discomforts associated with challenged or at least unshared beliefs and moral standards are evident in these responses:

I found few people who embraced my religious and moral standards and thus felt lonely. I wanted the fellowship of people of similar likes. I found this at Spring Arbor College, a Christian college operated by the Free Methodist Church.

Many people I knew were tasting freedom for the first time. They went cuckoo over it, joined "causes" they never understood, fell in love with people who were really sick, and tried to find their identity in some alley. I did too, for awhile, but I couldn't force myself to do it for long; thus, I found myself alone on Saturday night . . . . I am convinced that I had chosen the right thing to do. Go away!

I had an unhappy experience with a boy I thought I loved. He took advantage of the situation. I decided to come home.

Value confrontation can also lead to a considered change of values or a purposeful search for new possibilities. For example, a man, after three quarters in an experimental residential college program that attracted atypical students, after a long description of his sheltered, "clean-cut," attitudes in high school and first quarter at the university, had this to say about his leaving:

So I first came here caught under the impression that I had to go to college, get an education, a job, married, and stay in that little rut. Coming here introduced me to a completely different type of person. I think this exposure to radically different people and ideas has been the best thing that's ever happened and I don't think it would have happened outside Res Prog [a residential program]. I could have chosen a dorm, but there I would encounter a lot of bullshit and could once more choose my own group, whereas here the opportunity is so much greater to know other people that you can't really avoid it. The small classes with the profs right where you live makes a big impression. You'd never get that anywhere else . . . I guess I finally realized how ignorant I was and so I've decided to quit school awhile and go to work. This decision came about because I could see school was doing me no good and I've met so many different kinds of people and have seen what they've done.

CIRCUMSTANCES

There are obviously times when students simply find themselves the victims of circumstances, when matters largely beyond their control converge, when the institution has little if any role to play:

I got ripped off for some money, so I had to trace down the person who took the money. I missed three days of school and my teacher gave assignments every day so I was hopelessly behind—besides that I was working nights at Boeing, selling dope (which is a full time job) and trying to go to school at the same time—school wasn't bringing me anything but headaches, so I quit.

I got pregnant. My boyfriend finked out on me. My parents were getting a divorce. I am in California to have the baby. I love the college and will return.

I'm poor, but not poor enough to qualify for financial aid so I can never make it through a quarter of college because I run out of money to live on. When I have a job and go to school, both my job and schoolwork suffer because I need at least nine hours sleep a day and I can't get it. I'm going to work for awhile and try again.

According to the record I failed and was asked to leave, but I think you will understand the problem when you know my father had died suddenly on the day of my graduation from high school. While I was at college my closest uncle died of cancer. Then my boyfriend broke up with me soon after the beginning of the second semester. I couldn't concentrate on my studies. I tried, but I couldn't.

In order to describe more clearly the human dimension and to reinforce the multifaceted nature of student withdrawal, perhaps the description of characters, places, and reasons in their perspectives will clarify the whole issue of attrition.

Ernie, a student attending a technical-professional college in a small southern college, gave the following answer to the question, "Why are you withdrawing from college?":

Well, there are a lot of reasons why I'm withdrawing. Some of them are for academic, some of them are for purely social reasons. In coming to college I've had a certain purpose in mind, along with the kind of education and degree I wanted to attain. When I came here I came in good faith, but on the side I've had a lot of interference. I am from, socioeconomically, a poor background and I've had to work my way through the first year and a half of college. With loans and other different ways, I've been able to get myself through. But I've had a lot of interference from the Dean on this campus. There's a lot of question as to whether I would pay off my bills on time, and when I did ask for credit at one particular point when I was short—all I needed was an extension—it wasn't given to me. At that time I was dealt with a little roughly; the Dean addressed me with little respect. There were statements made to me and my parents which were, in my opinion, uncalled for. Even my mother was embarrassed on the phone by the Dean because he hung up on her while in the middle of a conversation. At one other time my father came to the college for a previously agreed on appointment. He stayed two days at a local motel and during all that time he was consistently refused the interview; so he went home a very angry man. That says something about the administration.

Another problem was that any information my parents received about my progress here during the semester came from me. At no time during my stay here did my parents receive any formal information from the college on my progress, except the grades at the end of the year.

As for the social problems, I had a boy draw a knife on me one time. I brought it to the dean and in the course of the conversation he made me feel very guilty. I realize that one is bound to have conflict in the dorms, tempers flare, and so on; but the way it was handled upset me.

At this college there are too many examples of professors getting on the back of students for what, to the professors, is unsound reasoning. [Southern students stressing economic exploitation of the South by the North.] For example, I remember a history professor who tried to educate us on the reasons why we had the Civil War. She used the old standby reason—to her, slavery was the only reason she could give, it seemed. We from the South know there were other reasons, but you hate to correct a PhD. It seems to me that so many of the professors here have a set of standard notes, not allowing innovation. If new things are discovered they don't seem to get to the classroom at this college.

Frank, who attended a very liberal Quaker college in the Midwest and intended to transfer to a larger institution, gave the following answer to the question, "why are you withdrawing from college?":

Well, its not that simple a question. I've learned quite a bit here. In this my second year here I realize that I don't especially like the atmosphere of the place. I find it very reactionary in comparison with other places I know of. And I want to go to a bigger place in a larger city because the city itself is one huge problem which is not the case in this small local community. So I want to be in a more cosmopolitan environment rather than the "hick" town that is here.

Another reason is that the school itself is completely controlled by the administration; the students have absolutely no power—I don't like that. That could be changed but it won't be, because the students around here don't seem to care.

There is another fairly important reason and that is that I want to go to a place which has a better program for me. I'm a pre-med student and their requirements which emphasize chemistry is not to my liking. I believe that at a larger institution I can get a more diversified program. But the academics here are not my main reason. If I liked the place I would stay.

Another student from the same college, Chris, gave several reasons for considering withdrawal that reflect the problem of a poor relationship between student and institution:

There are quite a few reasons. The first one that comes to mind is the idea that I don't feel I really fit in with the student body. I'm not sure I want to fit in with individuals here. I've noticed particularly that this place has become a collecting place for what I consider undesirable individuals, who I don't care to associate with. Even beyond just protesters, I find an awful lot of people here are unable to get along with anybody outside of their small group.

Another reason is that I'm a science major, and science more than any other field of study requires a vast range of ideas to be representative. At a small college such as this, where two full-time professors make up the entire science department, no matter how good or how bad they may be, I don't feel that it is adequate. From what is offered, I can't really get into the things which I like to study.

Faye, from the same college, showed similar feelings in answering the question, "Why are you leaving college?":

Well, there are a lot of reasons. The first reason is I prefer being in the East. I prefer being near a large city. I found out here that there's rarely anything to do on weekends that I enjoy—the movies are terrible. There are just things I can do in a large city that I can't do here.

The second reason is just the environment at this college. It's a great change from the East. It's a Midwest environment which I'm not used to at all. People here are very intolerant of any dissenting opinions—most are from Midwest. They object to other opinions in dress, in politics, or in anything else. This I don't like.

Another reason is that I've been having some personal problems here at the school, in my relationships with some of the kids. I want to go to a school where I don't have a particular reputation so I can start all over again. Actually, the personal problems that I have had brought my decision to a head, and I felt that it was best for me, academically and personally, to withdraw.

Paula, a black student attending a very conservative church-related college (Protestant), describes her reasons for leaving in terms of value orientations:

Actually my religion conflicts with that of the college. I don't want to take the Bible courses here which are required. It was strongly recommended by my priest not to take these courses. I am Catholic. Anyway, those courses are very boring. I suppose it is all right to be at this kind of an institution if you believe in the principles its founded upon, but when you must sit and have these views forced on you, it causes you to always be in the position of rebelling. Really, I can't think of anything this college has done for me. I have found no real friends here among the white people because most of the students and the faculty all think along the same lines.

I intend to transfer to Howard University and I'm sure this will be a positive change. I know I will meet many different kinds of people and fit in better in that kind of institution.

From the same institution was Gary, a student who wished to travel. He planned to go to Switzerland in order to expand his experiences, and gave the following reply to the question, "Why are you leaving college?":

Well, the religious atmosphere here is too stifling. The rules are really a bother. I am looked upon here as a "crackpot" because I've broken so many of the rules and had been caught by the administration. The consequence of this was that there had to be these long discussions with people on the administration about rule enforcement and the basic Christian reasons why they were necessary. It's my view that these rules are too strictly enforced and they really can't be enforced anyway. It seems to me on this campus that there is a mistaken idea of what a Christian really is. So many are Christians because they have a long list of things they follow—no dancing, drinking, smoking—yet that seems to be as far as it goes. Actually there are too many people here who profess Christianity, but cannot get along with anyone else. They are Christians with bad dispositions. But the rules are my biggest complaint.

Even where value orientations of the student are congruent with the institution, other reasons for withdrawal develop. Reuben, a Mennonite attending the same college, gave the following reason for leaving:

There's practically only one reason: because the college does not have my major. I've talked to some people here about going elsewhere, taking courses, then transferring back to graduate, but they are not willing to allow me to do that. So I must go to a school that can give me what I want.

I'm sorry to leave because the college is a good school. I came here with the intentions of having a spiritual emphasis which has been pretty good, but there are so many students here who couldn't care less about that—it hurts the religious program.

Students who attend the liberal-experimental colleges operate in a different sort of environment. They experience more freedom, both academic and social; they experience more emotional upheaval, they are less accepting of norms; and the emphasis in these colleges is on experiential learning.

Jane planned to leave her college for at least one semester to attend another school. Her reasons for leaving were fairly well thought out. She was an interesting mixture of doubt and confidence. She wanted to broaden her experience by learning in a new environment. She wanted to attend a conventional school to test her ability to meet the more rigorous requirements and standards as opposed to the experience she has had of setting her own. In response to the question, "Why are you leaving?", she replied:

I'd just like to study at another institution—maybe at a large university or in another country. Just to prove to myself that I can do well elsewhere, perhaps a place where you don't know your teachers so well, where the standards are set. Don't misunderstand, I really like the way of learning here, because it really suits me. I just want to see if I can do it some place else—a kind of self-proving thing.

I think that because I haven't been to another college before, I think it might be a good idea just to see what a lecture is like and just to see what a huge class is like. I may hate it, but it might be very interesting. No one here will tell you what it is like, you have to go out, then come back and tell them. I have a lot of doubts about the whole thing, still I've got to do it.

Steve, another student from the experimental college, withdrew for different reasons. Even though he had the opportunity to learn experientially, he sensed the need for more experience, but in a different context:

"Are you planning to leave college?"

"Yes, I am."

"Why?"

"To get away."

"To get away from what?"

"To get away from this school, and at least take a break; to get a job, to get a house of my own, and to do what the outside world does. I'm not getting much out of this college right now. I just want to get to the outside world. I'm going to live, I'm going to do. I don't want a profession; I want a life.
I've got a cabin in Maine. I'm going there for a while. I want to get out and think about me, to think about where I want to go next year. I'm done with my education as far as I can see."

"Has anyone influenced you in this decision?"

"Everybody has. Everything around me has influenced my decision. I want to do something. This is really an easy place not to do work, and, on the other hand, it's a hard place to do it. It's a place of extremes. I don't like it."

"I'm creative, I like to work with my hands. I am oriented to art—the creative arts. I'm interested in jewelry, painting, sculpture, working with films and things, but there are too many distractions on this campus to do these things. Anyway, you don't need to go to college to do what I want to do. This is what I think."

These examples illustrate the multifaceted condition of student attrition. Individual students present different reasons and any attempt to quantify student withdrawal on the basis of specific variables defeats the purposes of solutions based on that quantification. It is often said

that to fight massive trends or conditions is to welcome frustration. The
Eskimo lives with his climate, not against it. The sailor uses the wind to
make progress against it. An effective institution, of whatever character, should recognize these variables and make modifications to allow
for them.

In these illustrations, virtually all the students made a poor choice;
however, most of the original decisions were based on one or more legitimate reasons. It was only after experience within each community
that these students realized their first choice was not really the best one
for them. These illustrations further point out that the reasons given
were, for the leavers, quite legitimate. And probably they were wise decisions.

Ernie and Frank obviously were having difficulties with the bureaucracy, financial problems on the one hand and administrative domi-
nance on the other. Ernie and his parents were frustrated with the insensitivity of the dean to the very practical family problems of financing the higher educational experience. For them to be ignored was in-
excusable. Frank, though upset by the lack of student power, placed the
blame as much on students as on the administration. They both needed
help from unresponsive communities.

Chris was concerned about the quantity of teaching resources, while
Ernie was very much disposed to criticizing quality of teaching. In
Chris' case, the correction of his perceived problem was seen in the
movement to another environment. Ernie was disillusioned, not only
with the administrative insensitivity, but with the rigidity of the faculty.

Paula, Jane, and Steve were looking for identity and competence. The
only path for them was to seek these in a new environment, since they
were uncomfortable in their particular college communities. They
needed a change in order to satisfy internal needs which it seems only
they could resolve. Paula needed to be among people she could understand and who could understand her. Jane needed to prove something
to herself which could not be done in the environment in which she
found herself—her own sense of competence depended on another actual experience as it was not one that could be gained vicariously.
Steve wanted some sense of accomplishment through action.

Faye, Paula, and Gary were having problems with their own value
systems in relation to those of the institutions they were attending.
Faye could not understand the provincialism of the Midwest and what
she perceived as intolerance; *she* could not *tolerate* the local intolerance. Paula resented being placed in the position of rebellion against
the imposition of others' "superficial" values. Gary could not relate
what he knew of Christianity with rules supposedly based on that phi-

losophy. He was seeking what it means to be Christian apart from those man-made rules that were not congruent with his own internalized orientations. All three were experiencing value confrontation and taking steps to allow for their resolution.

Obviously, circumstances cannot easily be controlled. Circumstances are always with us, forcing us in directions which are not necessarily productive—this applies to students and nonstudents alike. What can be said about circumstances, except that both students and institutions should guard against using such phenomena to excuse weakness or lack of resolve?

This chapter begins with comments concerning the human dimension of the dropout phenomenon. We show through specific illustrations how the feelings, experiences, and perceptions of leavers influence withdrawal decisions. The questionnaires and interviews from which these illustrations were taken invariably surfaced such forces. And although it is neat to be able to set statistical significance on particular variables in many and varied studies, the failure of such studies, to this point, to significantly effect a change in the percentages of students withdrawing from institutions suggest that such studies are not meeting the needs of American youth in the context of their higher educational experience. Perhaps those percentages should not change; perhaps in view of universal higher education in the United States this is the level of "efficiency" we can and must accept. In fact, the dropout phenomenon could be the salvation of American education because it forces, among other things, educators to ask if they really believe in providing educational opportunity tailored to the educational development and individual needs of each youth (Beford, 1967).

We suspect that persistence in college requires the personal touch that only dedicated *professors* can give. Evidence, both personal and other, reveals that such dedication exists in abundance across America, but we further suggest that at the present time, it is largely misdirected. Teacher roles must become more personalized in order to satisfy both the academic and personal needs of students, thus relieving the tension between people and institutions that cause separation.

But now we are getting ahead of ourselves in the presentation. We are discussing implications, yet there is more to attrition than discussed so far.

CHAPTER FOUR

THE PROCESS
OF WITHDRAWAL

For some, the process of withdrawing from college is a painful experience, marked by self doubts, disappointment and depression; for others it is a positive step taken with confidence and conviction. Whether the process of leaving college results in something positive greatly depends on the "attitude" of the institution, reflected not only by the faculty, counselors, staff, and administrators, but also through the procedures for withdrawal and reentry. This chapter presents information pertaining to a series of related questions: What first precipitated the idea to withdraw? When did it occur? What feelings accompanied discussion and the final decision? With whom was the idea discussed? At what point along the way? How did the decision become solidified? What was the effect of various responses by college, parents, and friends?

Two Project on Student Development publications (Hannah, 1969b; Chickering and Hannah, 1969) described the process of withdrawal with freshman leavers and with potential sophomore dropouts. That study is expanded here to include leavers over a four-year period.

Data concerning the process of withdrawal came from the following: (a) an Institutional Classification Sheet (IC) (illustrated in Appendix D) completed by 13 colleges in the fall of each school year from 1966 through 1969 for each of 1256 students who did not return to college; (b) an Attrition Questionnaire (AQ) (Appendix E) sent to these students (leavers), and returned in useable form by 60 percent of them; and (c) 153 on-campus interviews with students who indicated they would be unlikely to enroll the following fall. Thus information during the withdrawal process was recorded as well as data gathered after the fact.

The following illustrations taken from interviews with potential leavers, as those in the previous chapter, to some degree capture the intricacies of thought and the varied pressures relative to withdrawal decisions.

JIM

"Are you definitely planning to leave college?"

"Yes."

"According to the form you filled out, you were. I wondered if you had changed your mind?"

"No, I'm definitely leaving."

"Why are you planning to withdraw?"

"Well, it's not that simple a question. I've learned quite a bit here. This is my second year at college and I now realize that I don't especially like the atmosphere, the general atmosphere of the place. I find it very reactionary in comparison to some of the places I've been. I want to go to a bigger college in a larger city because this town is against the college. Several times people in the town have beat up our students. It's just unpleasant to feel unwanted. So I want to go to a more cosmopolitan community.

And the school itself, I find, is completely controlled by the administration, the students have absolutely no power. I don't like that. I think that could be changed, but it won't be, because the students around here don't seem to care about it. Those are basically the reasons, but there is another fairly important one. The college I'm transferring to has a slightly better program. I'm a premed student and the program here requires that I either major in chemistry or biology. Right now, I'd rather get more of the liberal arts and then move on to the preprofessional requirements.

"How did you go about deciding to withdraw from this college? I mean, other than what you've told me that you don't think the sequence of courses is what you want for your premed program?"

"Well, I discussed it with several friends, with my parents. I haven't here at the college much. I did talk to the Dean of Men very briefly. My parents were involved quite extensively, and my friends. I didn't discuss it with any faculty members per se, because academics is not really the main gripe. Actually, academics here are pretty good. If I really liked the place I would stay."

"In other words you would say that the college personnel didn't really help you much in making your decision?"

"No, I didn't talk hardly at all with them."

"Why?"

"I didn't see that it was important to talk with them about it. It was a very personal decision, and I didn't want to bring everyone into it."

"What was the general attitude that you found among your peer group about your decision?"

"Some were surprised, but the great majority understood, and in the process I found that there's a great discontent among students here.

Some of my friends are transferring, and quite a few of them wished they could, but their grades are not high enough, so they can't without great loss."

"How do your parents feel about your proposed transfer?"

"Well, they understand what it's all about. We talked about it, and they gave me arguments pro and con, and I think they are very much behind me. They say that if I'm not happy, they want me to go somewhere where I think I'll be happy. They are really behind me."

"What kind of feelings do you have about yourself in relation to your decision to withdraw. Have you any misgivings?"

"No, I have no misgivings particularly. Oh, I don't like the idea of transferring because I'm going to have to go out and meet new people and everything. But I realize that at this point it's a thing that's really necessary. This college is not going to change, and if it doesn't I'm not going to keep growing. To stay here means that I will continue to resent the fact that the college is this way; that would interfere with my growth."

SUE

"Why don't you just start talking about why you are considering withdrawing—or how you decided to withdraw?"

"Well, the number one reason is that I'm getting married in August. That's a pretty good reason."

"Yes, a pretty good reason."

"The boy I'm engaged to is graduating in about five days and I think it would be difficult for me to be at college and him to be in Chicago as a teacher. So I plan to go and take my course at a school there. Maybe not this coming semester, but soon, so that I can finish my education. But right now we've got to get adjusted to each other and he's got to get adjusted to his job. Then when we get on our way I'm going to night school. I've had about three or four offers to teach kindergarten already—with just two years of education—so if I get that type of job I'll work from about 9 AM to 3 PM. That would be enough to take a couple of courses in the afternoon."

"So you're really not planning to discontinue college—basically it's the marriage?"

"Right."

"Then there's not too much to say about how you decided to withdraw from college?"

"Well, that wasn't a decision for me to make because he told me that—I—when we first discussed it I didn't want to finish school here, but I had to make a decision, if it was to be marriage now, or wait, or what. So I finally made my decision this one weekend when I went to my girl friend's house and her mother was trying to tell me to finish my education and wait a couple of years to get married. Well, I was pretty much swayed by her. Her husband had died and if she hadn't had her education she would have been left supporting three kids with no money. This was on Friday. Then on Sunday we went to visit one of her aunts. All of her life she saved her money so that when she became 65 she could take all this money and retire. She waited all her life to have this happiness and then two years after she retired she was crippled in an accident. She's in a wheelchair with no way to spend this money and have a good time and see the world. So I decided, why let happiness pass me by now, because there'd be a chance that if I continued school that something might happen. So I decided that I could have my cake and eat it too—get married and then go to night school. So that's how I decided. It was through that one weekend incident."

"How would you describe the academic atmosphere here?"

"First of all, the academic atmosphere here needs a lot of improvement. The professors here, some of them, I could get up and teach a class better than they do. I sincerely believe it. Because they don't take an interest in the school. And the school, as far as I feel, their main objective is to get money. I mean, most any business is, but there aren't enough dedicated people here to really make this school a success. And I think that's why so many kids leave this school. That's why this school is a suitcase school. Everybody goes home on weekends."

"Now that it's all decided, how do you feel about your decision to leave?"

"I think I made a wise decision. But then again, sometimes I think, I have the ability and everything, am I cutting myself short? Is marriage, can it be compared to an education in the sense of what it will give me? But then again I think it will. So I think I'll be satisfied. In fact I know I'll be satisfied being married, but sometimes I'm afraid I'll look back and say, 'I sure wish I had graduated from college.' But then again maybe I can appease myself by saying that I've had two years instead of nothing. . . . I don't think I can compare an education and love and marriage. I just can't compare going to this college and getting married."

BILL

"Have you definitely decided to withdraw?"

"Yes. I will be coming back, however, in two years. This is my plan at present anyway."

"And why are you considering withdrawing?"

"It's mainly in order to do my 1-W[1] work. However, this wasn't the motivating factor in my decision to take two years to put into practice

---

[1]Alternative service option in the Selective Service System.

what I find. My major is religion, and so I would like to take a break for two years and learn. I hope that these next two years of my 1-W work will be a classroom the very same way that the two years here have been, and that I feel I'll be—I'll know more exactly what I want when I come back."

I plan to work in a mission in San Francisco and will be taking up something very similar to a student pastorate, and I (will) work in the Youth Fair and in the mission program. That's one reason why I hope it's as much a classroom as it's been here, because it'll be a direct experience along the field that I'm interested in, working with young people and children, and going into the city, helping and so forth."

"How did you go about making your decision?"

"It just originated within myself. I mean there was no one who necessarily talked with me. I, uh, perhaps you could say that, uh, I just feel that next year I would have Greek and so forth, more of the stronger courses, the courses that I would have to know exactly what I'm doing and what is coming now. As of right now, I'm not really exactly sure, and so I think it was mainly this uncertainty."

"Whom have you talked to about these matters?"

"You mean if anyone counseled with me as to—actually no one. In fact, as far as making the decision goes, I didn't even talk it over with my parents too much. I simply told them that this was what I was thinking about. I knew that they would approve because they've always left me with my own decisions. I know that they approved of what I'm doing and so I simply made the decision and told them, and as far as counseling, if anyone here at the college, any faculty or anyone, I can't say that I even talked it over with any of them. Not even the faculty advisor that I have. I didn't even know him. I didn't even know who he was the first year. So this has been a decision of my own pretty much."

"How about friends?"

"I did talk to other guys—at least five or six—who had taken 1-W work. Other friends did have an influence—the guys who did their 1-W work before they came to college and so forth. . . . They felt this (idea) was best, they would have rather that they did it at the middle or at the end."

"When did you make the decision?"

"I would say about the middle of the year, at midsemester."

"Are there any other peripheral reasons for you planning to withdraw?"

"Perhaps, financially would be somewhat, although I've never let finances worry me; but this is a factor. . . . Perhaps my grades were not the best, but, uh, I could do a lot better here than I'm doing. I feel that I'll be able to do a lot better when I get back."

"What are the general attitudes of your friends, your peers?"

"Perhaps at the first I guess they reacted. 'Oh, why are you doing that? Get your education out of the way.' But then after they understand the situation better, I think . . . they see my reasoning."

"How do your parents feel about it?"

"They go along 100 percent I think. . . . I know exactly whenever I'm doing something that they don't approve of, and I haven't felt at all that they disapproved of this. They've left this to me."

"Could you say anything about the administration, the president, the deans, what have they meant to you?"

"They—there is a—a person can't feel relaxed with them and in their presence, and a person can't talk to them and feel free to go to them. They're interested in the stuff that they—but you can't feel free to talk to them, and yet they don't go out of their way to come to you, and they don't go out of their way to be. . . . I feel at times that they're kind of out for their own gain . . . perhaps it's just that they're too busy to really . . . to come down to the student's level and just talk and everything. But at times they seem quite distant and at other times not."

"Well, how do you feel about your decision?"

"Quite satisfied and quite resigned to the fact that I feel that this is what I should do for the experience and for the education aspect of it."

Arthur Chickering, who advised us on this chapter, provided an interpretation of the situations of such potential dropouts as Jim, Sue, and Bill. He explained:

"Jim's discomfort with the college environment and peers has sparked his thinking about and looking toward greener pastures. A feeling of not being wanted or needed in the community, directs his mind to a more cosmopolitan school and city where chances of finding a group more to his bent and liking are attractive. However, his frustration with the program and the seeming unwillingness of the college to change or make adjustments to it are also a factor in his decision. But he admits that he would stay if he could really like the place. Very significant in his point that he was not inclined to seek the counsel of faculty or administration—he did not feel it would be productive. Sue, balancing the emotional appeal of marriage against the logic of further education, torn by the drag of former styles and values and the pull of higher hopes and aspirations recently glimpsed, attracted by some aspects of the college and repelled by others, was pushed toward closure by the chance juxtaposition in one brief weekend of forceful arguments expressing both sides of her ambivalence. She opted for the one last heard. Bill, uncertain about his ability to cope with the more difficult courses of the junior and senior years, uncertain about his choice of program, unable to connect with college faculty or administration for significant relationships, is shifting toward more liberal religious views and needs to complete alternate service. Leaving for a period of work consistent with future vocational plans both delays decisions and provides a better basis for resolving current ambiguities."

Yes, complex person-institution-life style dynamics like these are but feebly captured by numbers, and generalizations are like Procrustes, lopping of some students' tops, bottoms, or both, and stretching others. Jim, Sue, and Bill clearly are not typical cases. But again, we ask, "What student is?"

COLLEGE REPORTS AND LEAVER REPORTS

The *college reports* revealed that leavers most frequently left voluntarily with an adequate (often marginal) grade point average. Few were behavior problems and few expected to return to the particular college from which they withdrew. The college was ignorant of most of their plans. Emotional difficulties, absence of clear objectives, and goals different from the college—along with marriage—were often seen by the college as the major reasons for withdrawal. According to the colleges, some leavers also found the work difficult, some were dissatisfied with the faculty or college, and some could not pursue the program they wanted. The college reports shed little direct light on the withdrawal process.

The *leaver report* forms mailed to all withdrawn students generated more complex and comprehensive data. Respondents confirmed college reports that most leavers voluntarily withdraw with adequate grade point averages. More leavers reported themselves as troublesome, and twice as many leavers said they were transferring than was indicated by the colleges. A significant finding was that *the colleges knew nothing about where 49 percent of the leavers were going and what they would be doing*—a disappointing commentary on the college's withdrawal procedures. The most important determinants of withdrawal reported by these leavers were: academic underachievement or difficulty, discrepancy between the college's professed beliefs and its actual behavior, dislike of the general college atmosphere and activities, hearing about another school that seemed better, and a general feeling of discomfort.

According to leavers, for 23 percent of those who withdrew during the four years, first thoughts of leaving took place in June, May, or January in that order. Final decisions to leave occurred at similar times— June (51 percent), May (14 percent) and January (10 percent). Among all respondents, *77 percent reported that their final decisions came either during the summer vacation or during the times the college was not in session.*

Barger and Hall (1964b) suggest that the stress under which students operate at the end of the semester is conducive to thoughts of withdrawal; thus the actual decision to leave is made while students are away from the campus, when pressures to remain may be low, when feelings of relief are high, and when other practical and noncollegiate influences are often more strongly felt (cf. Hannah, 1969c).

Related to the final decision, but specifically connected to first thoughts about withdrawal, was the finding that almost *25 percent of all leavers first considered leaving the colleges even before their actual enrollment as first year students occurred,* suggesting a large degree of uncertainty about attending college at all, or preplanning which excluded graduation from the college of first matriculation.

Leavers were asked to indicate topics which came up for discussion as withdrawal was considered. Of 20 alternatives, the 10 most *frequently* mentioned in rank order were:

1. Academic underachievement or difficulty.
2. Educational plans and purposes.
3. Vocational plans.
4. Religious beliefs.
5. Attitudes and values.
6. Financial problems.
7. Plans concerning life in general.
8. College rules and regulations.
9. Limited offering in college programs.
10. Educational opportunities elsewhere.

Topics infrequently discussed were problems with friends of the same or opposite sex or difficulty with peers in general, problems with faculty members or college authorities, problems with parents, marriage, and pregnancy.

PERSONS GIVING COUNSEL AND THEIR REACTIONS

Most of those whom the leavers approached most often about withdrawal were reported to be warm and understanding—parents (76 percent), friends (67 percent), deans and faculty (29 percent), counselors (10 percent), and psychologists and pastors (7 percent). Real efforts to help came mostly from parents (77 percent) and friends (54 percent); however, college personnel were also helpful, but less frequently (47 percent). Counselors rated least helpful. In fact, potential leavers' assessment of college advising suggests the need for colleges to carefully assess the need and performance of most counseling programs. Students seem to be saying to us in higher education that counseling and advising systems are not working well.

Most of those whom the students approached urged them to persist in college, except college counselors who rarely advised persistence. It also seemed evident, judging from student comments, that leavers tend to perceive deans and administrators as those who are clearly more interested in the college than in problems of the leavers. For each topic of discussion, the Attrition Questionnaire offered 11 options: friend of the same sex, friend of the opposite sex, father, mother, brother or sister, teacher, dean or administrator, college counselor, psychologist-psychiatrist, pastor, and other. With two exceptions, each of the top 10 topics was discussed in greater frequency with friends *and* parents. One exception was religious beliefs which were discussed principally with peers and seldom with parents; pastors, college personnel, and others were not involved at all. The other exception was financial problems; they were discussed with parents, but infrequently with others. Leavers seldom discussed with college personnel limitations in college curricula, extracurricular activities, or such matters as religious beliefs, attitudes and values, plans concerning life in general, and financial problems. They did discuss academic underachievement, educational and vocational plans, college rules and regulations, and educational opportunities elsewhere with college personnel.

Thus discussions about withdrawal issues as Table 4.1 shows were mainly with friends and parents. Among friends, a friend of the same sex participated first, then came a friend of the opposite sex. Faculty were consulted, but at less than half the frequency of parents and peers. Deans, administrators, and counselors were seldom involved in discussions of leaving, and psychologists and pastors almost never.

LEAVERS' ATTITUDES ABOUT SELF, COLLEGE, AND SOCIETY

There is much diversity in leavers' feelings toward themselves, their colleges, and society as a whole. In general, students admit directly that they are angry at neither the system of higher education nor society. Neither are they especially anxious, disappointed, angry, or uncertain about themselves or their decision. Only a small percentage of leavers seem ambivalent about the decision to leave. In fact, the outcomes of the decision and subsequent experiences seem quite positive.

TABLE 4.1 THE PROCESS: WITH WHOM DO THEY TALK?

Area of Concern	Whom Do They Talk With Most Often?	Who Is Also Significant, If Anyone?	Who Is Clearly Not Significant?
Academic difficulties	Peers	Parents and college personnel	Counselors
Religious beliefs	Peers	No one	Parents, pastors, and college personnel
Financial difficulties	Peers	Parents	College personnel
Attitudes and values	Peers	Parents and college personnel	College personnel
Limitations in curriculum or extra curricular activities	Peers	No one	College personnel
Educational opportunities elsewhere	College personnel	No one	Parents
College rules and regulations	College personnel	No one	Parents

Consistently the leavers refer to expressions of independence, reassessment, and experiential learning.

INDEPENDENCE

Finally, I am able to do what I want.

I am free to do anything I want without breaking college rules.

I felt forced to do many things I didn't want to do. I am on my own and feel free to develop as a person.

The college was my parents' choice—now I am shaping my own future instead of my parents shaping it for me.

I am free to be me.

I am happier in my new found freedom and independence than I was in the strict confines of college; independence also shows me obligations and responsibilities.

REASSESSMENT

I needed to grow up and I did. I discovered that I hadn't been ready for college.

I am happier, less nervous, and have learned more about life in general from my experiences than any book could have taught me. Colleges are useful for some people. My temperament and attitudes were not suitable to the college environment. College is not for everyone, no matter what college faculties say.

I now know where I am headed and have chosen my profession.

I have become more certain of my future plans. It has given me the time away from college that I needed.

It [withdrawal] has brought some of life's rich rewards to me.

EXPERIENTIAL LEARNING

It helped me to realize the importance of college and how very much I wanted to go. Now I am ready to go back.

It was wise to withdraw and wise to return. A year away from school helped me discover that even if it was hard work, it was a lot better than anything else I could do. I know now that I can do college work; I think I was just not ready for it before.

I continually understand more of the expectations of a college and how they coincide with my own expectations, and I have a chance to experiment with different jobs. I will return.

My temporary withdrawal, through travel and life abroad, I developed an enthusiasm for learning about places and people. Confidence in myself was increased.

I feel I have matured, and will be a better person to continue my education at a later date.

I matured and fortunately had the opportunity to go to another college.

I plan to go back to college because I now realize my potential and what I am and ought to do with it. I now enjoy my work but realize its limitations. I hope this period of adjustment will better prepare me for my future education that I am now sure I must have.

I found ideals, beliefs which I wanted, plus goals for college. Going to college will now be more relevant and meaningful . . . I could not see these when I was there.

The data from colleges when compared with student responses are particularly important because they reveal institutions actually know little about those students who decide to leave. Little effort, apart from collecting cursory statistics, is made during the school year to identify potential leavers. And even when colleges discover that relatively large percentages of the enrolled have left, they make only small efforts to discover the "reality" of the leavers' action. At exit interviews, inadequate information was collected and most of those who withdrew were not accounted for at all regarding why, how, or where. For instance, colleges reported that 25 percent of leavers were transfers, while 52 percent of students leaving indicated they were transferring to another college. Discrepancies between what colleges knew about their dropouts and what the dropouts said fell into categories such as voluntary and involuntary withdrawal, academic performance, behavior patterns, expectations, and what the leavers planned to do and where they planned to go.

The general picture of minimal interaction is especially unfortunate for two reasons. First, for most students the decision to leave becomes final in June or even in May. January is the next most frequent month. Closure, therefore, occurs at the end of the semester or shortly after leaving. Prior discussions with college personnel can enlarge the range of issues considered by leavers, parents, and friends, can expand perspective concerning future alternatives and consequences, and can deepen insight concerning past and present forces at work. In short, they can help the concerned persons work toward a wise decision based on sound information thoroughly considered. The opportunities for such discussions remain open throughout the semester. For most students this could avoid the loss of additional advice part way through their firm and final decisions.

Whenever discussions with college personnel are held, students find them valuable. That is the second reason to decry minimal interaction. Tabulations from the interviews with potential leavers indicate that 65 percent of those planning to transfer and 72 percent of those not transferring, when they had a discussion with college personnel, found it valuable or fairly valuable. These figures compare favorably with those for parents and peers; about 75 percent of transferring and nontransferring students rated discussions with them valuable or fairly valuable. So college personnel *can make* valuable contributions. But prevailing institutional climates and student-faculty and student-counselor relationships—for reasons not yet clearly understood—lead to minimal interaction. Thus the potential benefits are realized by but few students. The answer, as we point out more fully in the last chapter, may lie with increased faculty sensitivity and accessibility.

CHAPTER FIVE

WHERE THEY GO, WHAT THEY DO, HOW THEY ADAPT

More is known about what happens to the university dropout, stopout, and transferee than is commonly believed. Furthermore, what is known suggests that we have been overestimating the negative implications of interrupted studies and even permanent dropping out. Frankly, no one has ever demonstrated that eight continuous semesters is the best way to get educated.

First, we know that a large proportion of those who withdraw from the college of first enrollment either return (stopout) or transfer to another institution within a short time of withdrawing. Second, a large proportion of the reenrolling students earn the intended degree and many go on to graduate school; in fact, Pervin (1966) found that dropouts from Princeton who went on for advanced degrees were as successful in obtaining the advanced degree as those who did not interrupt their studies. Most admissions personnel at small colleges report, on the basis of impression, that returning students do better than they did prior to stopping out. Third, the lifetime earnings of those not earning degrees is almost as high as the earnings of the college graduate; the extent of overlapping incomes is the significant indicator of success rather than the small difference in average incomes. Fourth, there is little evidence that dropping out temporarily or permanently has much, if any, long-term negative effect on a person's sense of self-worth, career choice, or success in marriage. Moreover, there is a growing body of findings that suggest leaving college is a positive step taken by individuals to constructively reevaluate important decisions. It may well be, as both the Carnegie and Newman reports suggest, that too many students continue uninterruptedly on to degrees without using enough of life as preparation for education. And finally, dropping out appears to be overrated as a problem in its own right; it is rather the result or symptom of other problems, often originating earlier in life (cf. Bachman et al., 1971, Farnsworth, 1957).

LATER ACADEMIC PERFORMANCE

Follow-up queries on withdrawn students from Princeton, Illinois, Michigan, the private colleges we have discussed elsewhere in this book, and even two English universities, all indicate that over half of the students reenroll somewhere, and approximately half of those reenrolling eventually earn degrees; in fact, Pervin (1966) concluded ". . . a returning dropout had a better chance of obtaining a baccalaureate degree than the average freshman had of obtaining the degree without becoming a dropout!" (p. 44).

The rate of returning to a college and then earning a degree somewhere varies considerably according to the "quality" of the institution, with the highest return and degree completion rates being at prestigious private universities, and lowest return and degree completion rates being at the community and junior colleges. Table 5.1 illustrates the estimated return rates and eventual degree completion rates for five types of institutions. The prestigious private colleges are the Harvards, Stanfords, and Princetons; the better public universities are the Michigans, Berkeleys, and Wisconsins; the typical state universities are those institutions that do not have national reputations; the state colleges are the typical regional public colleges. Private liberal arts colleges, often church-related, sometimes limited to men or women, are so diverse that normative statistics would be meaningless; therefore, no category for these colleges is included.

Table 5.1 illustrates the limited value of normative statistics that report on the nation's total dropout rate; the rate obviously appears to differ considerably according to type of institution. However, the *real difference* is according to the ability and the socioeconomic status of the student, for even within a particular institution the rate of return will be much higher among those having greater academic promise (higher GPAs and entrance test scores) and coming from higher socioeconomic class backgrounds. Thus, while there is no doubt the annual rate of withdrawal is high, it is not high among students of superior academic ability attending the better colleges and universities; and, even if these students withdraw, they are more likely to return to earn degrees than their less able peers.

Ability is the best indicator of the likelihood to return to higher education, but the cause of withdrawal is also a good indicator of whether the individual will return. Those citing marriage and job opportunities

**TABLE 5.1   LATER ACADEMIC PERFORMANCE OF STUDENTS WHO
WITHDRAW FROM THEIR COLLEGE OF FIRST MATRICULATION***

Type of Institution	Returning to College	Eventually Earning Baccalaureate Degrees
Prestigious private universities	90–95%	80–85%
Better public universities	80–85%	70–75%
Typical state universities	60–70%	50–60%
State colleges	40–50%	30–40%
Junior and community colleges	20–30%	10–20%

*These data were compiled from follow-up studies reported by Astin (1972 and 1975), Bayer (1973), Cope (1969), Hannah (1971), Newman (1971), and Pervin (1966).

are least likely to return, whereas students who claim they quit because of lack of goals or personal problems are most likely to return.

Academic failure has much less effect on eventually completing college if the failure is at an institution with a "quality" image than if the failure is from an institution with less academic stature. In the first instance, the student usually simply transfers to another institution where the pressure for performance is not as great; in a surprising number of instances this will be to community colleges where a "retreading" occurs; many universities are surprised when they find they transfer more students *to* community colleges than they receive from the community college. Students experiencing academic failure, however, in the less selective institutions are not likely to continue in higher education, as they generally abandon any plans for a degree.

WOMEN ARE A SPECIAL CASE

It is clear that a woman is much more inclined to discontinue an academic program to follow a loved one, to raise a family, or to get married. Women are also more likely to leave college temporarily, usually to transfer, after a disappointment in a love affair. They are also more inclined than men to leave college when there is a financial, health, or personal crisis in the family: "I was needed at home to care for my mother;" "my brother's illness . . .;" "Dad could not take care of the children alone." Because of these circumstances, the woman is least likely to return.

However, the students of both sexes who give reasons for leaving that touch on "finding myself," "learning what is important in life," "needed time to grow up," "needing to get out of the unreal world (college)," almost always return, and there is a growing body of evidence suggesting that there are substantial benefits to those who drop out temporarily. They often return with a clearer sense of purpose, feeling more confident and competent.

I dropped out after my sophomore year because it didn't make sense to keep spending my parents' money when I wasn't sure about what I wanted to do with a degree. I tried newspaper work for a year and decided it wasn't for me (that was my major), then just bummed around southern California until I ran out of money which forced me to get a job—any job. After a couple of odd jobs, I found myself a place in a bookstore selling and helping customers—it was a real turn on; I mean, really helping people find what they want. I'm back now—in business administration. I want to go back to the book business, perhaps in sales—I think I will be happy there.

I love my courses for the first time; I'm not so concerned about post-graduate plans. I no longer feel so pressured by the atmosphere to be prepared for some high-powered career. I no longer see my undergraduate career as necessarily a direct preparation for graduate school, a profession or a career, and consequently I enjoy it just for what it is.

A RADCLIFFE SOPHOMORE[1]

OCCUPATIONAL ATTAINMENT

There is a pervasive assumption that a college degree is necessary for vocational success. Since those who have achieved the highest measures of recognition for their vocational endeavors have college degrees, those without degrees are clearly handicapped, are not likely to be productive, are failures, or at least have limited possibilities for success. In many ways the primary argument against dropping out is based on the likelihood of limited occupational attainment: the dropout gets the less attractive and less well-paid positions. This argument places emphasis on the degree as a credential.

The long-term follow-up studies of those dropping out permanently, or even for short periods of time, usually *do* find that the college graduate or the consistent persister earns more than the person who started, but did not earn the degree or stopped out. The differences in earning potential are not, however, nearly as large as most of us in higher edu-

[1]From "Where Did You Go? Out!" See Lindsay (1974).

cation assume them to be, or even consistently in favor of the college graduate. After comparing the annual income between dropouts and nondropouts for three classes of Princeton men, Pervin noted:

> While these data would tend to indicate a certain economic value in having a degree, a comparison of dropouts' salaries by No Degree, Degree, and Beyond Degree categories raises some puzzling questions. The No Degree dropouts are *not* consistently at a disadvantage. In fact, in the classes of '51 and '60, they (the No Degree dropouts) have higher mean and median incomes than either the Degree or Beyond Degree dropouts. In sum, while non-dropouts appear to earn more money than the dropouts, this cannot easily be attributed to the lack of a degree on the part of the dropouts (pp. 46–47).

In a footnote, Pervin explains that one plausible reason the nondegree earning dropouts reported higher incomes was that they went into business while many of the degree holders went into teaching.

Pervin is not alone, however, in finding a weak relationship between having a degree and vocational success: Kendall (1964) reported on the incomes of dropouts and nondropouts from two English universities, noting that while nondropouts earned more money than dropouts, the students who dropped out and returned to earn degrees (the stopouts) were earning less money than the permanent dropouts; Eckland (1964b) concluded that less than 20 percent of the variance in later vocational success could be accounted for by social class and college graduation combined; Bachman et al. (1971) compared the earnings of high school dropouts with high school graduates after controlling for length of time on the job and actually found the dropout was earning slightly more than the graduate; and, finally, while not directly related to the question, the conclusions drawn from *Education and Jobs: The Great Training Robbery* (Berg, 1970) and *Inequality: A Reassessment of the Effect of Family and Schooling in America* (Jencks, et al., 1972) are further indications that we place too much emphasis on degree completion as an indication of potential occupational attainment.

While this review has emphasized income as the measure of success, studies of wider varieties of adult accomplishment have found no relationship between adult accomplishment and conventional measures of college success. For example, in a large-scale follow-up investigation of college student careers, it is reported that adult accomplishments are uncorrelated with academic talent, including test scores, high school grades, and college grades (Munday and Davis, 1974).

Perhaps more important than earnings, specific position, or adult accomplishment is the satisfaction one has with whatever work he is doing. Even here neither the dropout from secondary school (Bachman, et al. 1971) nor the dropout from college (Pervin, 1966) has been found to be less satisfied.

LATER PERSONAL LIFE

After talking with and reading the responses from hundreds of students who have withdrawn from college, it is difficult to say that the experience of withdrawal has had any immediate or long-term negative effect on their sense of self-worth, their world views, or even their aspirations. The more able usually completed college somewhere because they knew they were "college material", while those who were uncertain about the value of college in the first place or who recognized their talents were not useful in the academic world went on to satisfying work, marriage, raising children, and became constructive citizens.

The initial effect of withdrawal is usually a sense of relief, followed by a brief sojourn:

> I am happier, less nervous, and I have learned more about life in general from my experiences than any book could have taught me. Colleges are useful for some people. My temperament and attitudes were not suitable to the college environment. College is not for everyone, no matter what the faculties say.

> My withdrawal was a wise decision, I have slowed down, looked around and re-evaluated. I desire to return with specific interests.

> I felt forced to do many things I didn't want to do. I am now on my own and feel free (because I'm responsible for me) to develop as a person—determining what I am to wear, how late I can stay out; small things, but they build up. I needed to read; I am able to invest reading time in what is relevant to my development.

> My withdrawal gave me the opportunity to get into the real nonacademic world. It gave me the chance to be totally disillusioned about my capacity for well-being without a college education. I was enabled to break away from my parental chains. The direction of my life became my responsibility, and for a while that direction did not include college.

> My withdrawal has given me the experience that I probably would never have had, or the opportunity to have again. It has given me a break from the academic pressures to consider more definite plans for the future, and to learn more about myself and other people, especially those of different cultural backgrounds.

For some, however, the first effect is shock, especially in cases where academic expectations were not realized, but the eventual outcome is to get back into some form of advanced training:

I want very much to say this. When I left college I was lost. I could not get a job that would be commensurate with my abilities. In short, I had no place to go. I was down and no one there to help me. Of course, it was my fault, I left and I suppose I have to pay the penalty.

When I first withdrew everything looked very dark and discouraging. Later after marriage and a good job the future looked very promising.

I thought I was doing the right thing at the time I dropped out, but I dreaded my decision. Like many things in life, a person doesn't realize the importance of something till he loses it. I'm thankful I have the opportunity to correct my mistake.

When I left school I felt I was doing a terrible thing, but later I felt it was the wisest thing I've done. One's life and environment are to a great extent in one's own hands in this society. I've found I'm generally capable of a great deal more than I thought I was. One's education depends for the most part on one's own willingness to learn—wherever he may be.

Withdrawal was a wise decision because while at college I had many thoughts as to whether or not I was pursuing the field in which I was or would be happy. Therefore, I thought by spending a few years away I would have a better understanding of what I really wanted. I hope to go back to school with a more mature and definite state of mind than the devastating feeling I had in college and at the time of my withdrawal.

Among the many patterns of experience after leaving, several tend to stand out. One common pattern is clearly purposeful, constructive adaptation. The student with high academic potential as evidenced by high school record, but who flunks out, will often with determination transfer to another "almost-as-good" college immediately, build a good academic record, and return to the original college or to one of equal stature. The student, often from an upper middle-class family, who begins to question the value of college, to wonder about his or her values, and has doubts about a vocational choice, will usually plan a dropout period for up to a year then reenroll. The stopout time is usually spent in some form of vagabonding, often in Europe. Students experiencing a severe disappointment in a relationship with a member of the opposite sex (usually women) simply transfer, usually to an institution closer to home. Students who become disenchanted with bureaucracy, teaching assistants, and the large university, simply enroll in a small college, while the small college student who wants anonymity and the excitement of the large urban community transfers to an urban college or a large university. Students without a strong academic record and lacking a commitment to a degree will usually simply find a job and not give the matter of more college much thought.

On the whole, then, we find patterns of behavior that are realistic and positively adaptive for the vast majority of youth. These students are not particularly disappointed in themselves or particularly anxious, but rather feel confident about their decision. They are not angry at society in general, at the college, at their parents, or at themselves, and they are not disillusioned with colleges in general. The large majority of students are making these constructive adaptations.

There are students, however, who leave and are neither happy nor unhappy about their future plans. They are not relieved to be leaving, even though they feel little uncertainty about their future plans. They are not uncertain about their abilities, but neither are they confident about their future performance. Thus they leave with mixed emotions:

> I have ambiguous feelings in regard to the objective value of my leaving college. Certain beneficial meetings and experiences have been made possible, and I think I have grown in maturity and openness of outlook. However, I still greatly desire an academic education; indeed, graduate school is included in my future plans.

For some students—fortunately, a small minority (about 5 percent)—the effect of leaving is clearly negative. Here we find the emotional exhortations, criticism, and rejection, both at the time of departure and years later. The initial effect is that of shock, depression, anger, and guilt:

> We all griped about academic weaknesses, disorganization, etc. But what actually shocked me, was not these things, which everyone knew existed, but the amazing dichotomy between professed attitudes and actual conduct of the administration. They enroll kids they cannot help, ignore their problems, merely to maintain the air of a School of Scholars. They must stop hiding their heads or others will leave just as I did.

> All of the professional people, both psychiatrists and school administrators to whom I have spoken about the details of my dismissal from college, agree that it was arbitrary and unwise. But more than that, it pointed up that need for responsibility to its students, that the college must satisfy. After my dismissal, I simply got very drunk, very morose, and scratched my wrists. Terrible! Violent! Yes, if you see it as a suicide attempt and not a plea for attention. . . . What the college does for students who endanger its image is evident in my case, in the irresponsible way I was shoved off-campus regardless of how upset I was about it. The procedures of a frightened, unprepared administration are very scary.

> I was too young, too idealistic, to handle the freedom and the choice necessary to actively participate in college life. Unfortunately, I feel that I am able to do so now and I feel guilty about giving myself a raw deal by leaving so abruptly. The withdrawal was definitely unwise. I would do almost anything to rescind that decision.

Years later, examples of effects include:

Since I have left the college I have come to feel that my withdrawal may have been an irreparable loss.

My sanity has nearly returned. I am in the same salary range as many of my friends who have graduated. I am not now a financial burden to my parents. I became rather unstable emotionally. My opinion of my college has cut off my desire to become further educated.

Since my withdrawal I have learned that the inadequacies were within me and not intrinsically within the environment of that institution.

I am much more stable emotionally and have more of a perspective on reality and what is important. I have satisfied the curiosity, or perhaps more accurate, the fascination, I had with beards and long hair—and of course, progressive education. If I am to return to college, I would not be susceptible to disappointment and disillusionment because of these last years utterly disheartening experiences.

Leaving school temporarily or even transferring immediately to a new college is obviously often a positive step to get out of an untenable situation or simply to reevaluate important issues and decisions about life. Our work and more recent studies (Kesselman, 1975; Lindsay, 1974; Wright, 1973) clearly suggest substantial short and long-term benefits of temporarily dropping out of college. Because we find little evidence of short-term or long-term negative effects from dropping out, we believe it is overrated as a problem in its own right. The negative results are more often the end result or symptom of other problems or of trends originating much earlier in life. Permanent dropouts experience difficulties. Their self-esteem, their aspirations, their vocational positions, their average incomes, their collection of certificates, is below some mean—an "average" that may not be important. But these limitations—family, personality, ability—are already present or predictable at the time of entering college and there is little evidence that dropping out makes matters worse. Colleges may, however, precipitate certain dropout behavior because of the stresses of examinations, grades, required credits, deadlines, because of the social demands, and because of the general environmental climates of very different colleges. We explore the effects on students of different colleges in the next chapter.

CHAPTER SIX

DIFFERENT COLLEGES, DIFFERENT PROBLEMS

When colleges differ from one another dramatically, and when their entering students are also diversified among themselves, it is reasonable to expect that the characteristics and problems of the dropouts would also vary from institution to institution. We find stopouts, dropouts, and transferring students from small, conservative, church-related colleges have different personality characteristics and problems than students from technical-vocational colleges, than students at liberal, experimental, "heathen" institutions, than students in the mega-, multi-, and megapopulist state universities. We illustrate some of these college and student differences by examining three real, but for our purposes pseudonymous, types of colleges: church-related (Simon, Savior, W.J.B., and Divinity); technology-related (Rocket and Stonewall); and liberal-experimental (Kildew and Classic).

We characterize the colleges first, then illustrate the general characteristics of all departing students, and finally illustrate how student leavers at the three types of institution differed from their peers who persisted at these same institutions. Two questions are answered: How do institutional goals and climates differ from campus to campus? How do characteristics of students who withdraw differ from those who remain? The colleges and data are from a study of student development of 13 small colleges referred to in the text as the Project (see Chickering et al., 1968; Chickering, 1969; Hannah, 1969b; Hannah, 1970c).

CHURCH-RELATED

The campus environment of the four small, conservative, church-related colleges is warm, friendly, and sympathetic. Faculty members, administrators, and students feel that they are a part of a community that has some coherence and cohesion, and that persons who are there care about each other and about the larger entity, the college. They are polite and considerate of one another, manners are important, and there are rather clear expectations concerning which behaviors are proper and which are not. There is limited emphasis on aesthetic or artistic awareness; social and political issues and national events do not penetrate the daily life in any complex or significant fashion; there is little preoccupation with personal problems and concerns. Carrying on serious scholarship is less important than being a solid and sound member of the community; how one behaves and fits in is more important to success and status than academic excellence alone.

The religious emphasis is a dominating press. Simon, Savior, W.J.B., and Divinity require daily chapel attendance and courses in religion, theology, and Bible studies. Faculty members must sign a statement indicating adherence to a religious creed as a condition of employment and prayer meetings are part of the week's routine. At Simon, for example, frequent prayer meetings among girls in the dorm are reported, "usually one big dorm prayer meeting per week, one small group (5–7) meeting per week, and one off-dorm prayer meeting per week." At Divinity, prayer meetings are held once a week, last about an hour, and are student planned, organized, and operated; hymn singing is followed by prayer and testimonials, and the meeting is ended with more prayer. Attendance, although voluntary, is taken seriously. The extent to which the religious convictions permeate life is revealed by the frequency of references to theology and religious beliefs in conversations with students and faculty and in some cases by the practice of opening classes with prayer or readings from the Bible.

TECHNOLOGY-RELATED

One of the two colleges emphasizing technical and vocational programs has substantial numbers of commuting students, while the other is almost totally residential and draws students from rural and conservative backgrounds. These colleges reflect even more limited concern for personal, artistic, and social awareness than do the church-related colleges. There are no established expectations concerning manners or proper behavior and there is much less sense of community.

LIBERAL-EXPERIMENTAL

At the two liberal-experimental colleges, which differ markedly from the other institutions, little attention is given to order, supervision, or

TABLE 6.1 MOST AND LEAST DESIRED CHARACTERISTICS OF GRADUATES

Pattern	Most Desired Characteristics	Least Desired Characteristics
Church-related	Educated in the liberal arts within the context of a Christian world view. Committed to Christ. Guided by God's will. Activated by Christian ideals in the various pursuits of life. Dedicated to Christian service.	Independent member of society Recognizes and accepts feelings as relevant to decisions. Education in the traditional liberal arts. Mixes easily but chooses friends carefully.
Professional-vocational	Prepared for future professional activities. Possesses skills and abilities for future vocation. Capable of effective judgment based on sound analyses of relevant information. Socially responsible and participating citizen. Constructive and creative member of interdependent society. Aware of the broad cultural foundations of our society.	Committed to Christ. Guided by God's will. Educated . . . within the context of a Christian world view. Activated by Christian ideals in the various pursuits of life. Independent member of society. Educated in the traditional liberal arts.

Liberal-experimental

Has understanding of self as an individual and as a member of society.
Constructive and creative member of interdependent society.
Capable of effective judgment based on sound analysis of relevant information.
Able to recognize and develop own creative potentials.
Socially responsible and participating citizen.
Aware of the broad cultural foundations of our society.
Activated by the intellectual, cultural, moral, and spiritual values of our civilization.

Committed to Christ.
Guided by God's will.
Dedicated to Christian service.
Educated . . . within the context of a Christian world view.
Mixes easily but chooses friends carefully.

practical concerns. There is a strong sense of community and recognition that persons care for each other and are standing together, although that sense is not as strong as at the small church-related colleges. Personal, social, artistic and aesthetic awareness is emphasized most, and scholarship is important only when it contributes to that awareness.

These three patterns suggest clusters of quite different institutions that are distinct from one another in major ways. Other Project findings concerning institutional characteristics fill out these differences as they are reflected in college objectives, student-faculty relationships, curriculum, teaching, and evaluation. Some of the differences were determined when members of each faculty and administration were given a College Goals Rating Sheet that listed 25 characteristics of graduates, and were asked to represent the objectives of their institution by indicating the two most desirable characteristics, the two least desirable, and then the five next most desirable and the five least so. Table 6.1 gives the results for the colleges. The church-related colleges are remarkably similar not only in the characteristics most desired, but in those least desired. Whenever an item had an explicit religious referent it was ranked high by all four colleges. When these items are compared to those for the other colleges, it should be recognized that faculty members and administrators at the church-related colleges think that the intellectual, social, and professional-vocational dimensions of the other patterns are expressed within the five items they ranked highest. Indeed, how the graduate who is committed to Christ differs in behavior from the secular graduate who is strongly committed to a similar value system that has a humanistic basis is often unclear. The difference has real meaning for faculty and for many students at church-related colleges, but clear communication of that difference to someone outside the community is sometimes difficult to achieve.

At Rocket and Stonewall Colleges, the emphasis on professional and vocational preparation is clearly reflected, together with a concern for general intellectual competence and social awareness. Kildew and Classic emphasize characteristics predominantly related to personal development, intellectual competence, social awareness, and responsible citizenship.

These differences in objectives were supported by more detailed information when three-man teams traveled to each campus and talked to students, faculty members, and administrators to obtain more concrete information about the programs and practices at these colleges. They went to classes, chapels, assemblies, ball games, and visited dormitories, snack bars, and cafeterias. Judgments based on brief visits are risky, yet their reports are consistent with the characteristics and emphases indicated by College and University Environment Scales (CUES) and goal statements.

One visitor, for example, reported a very warm and friendly atmosphere at W.J.B., one of the church-related colleges where there was a strong feeling of community.

One needs to be on campus only a short time to sense a strong community spirit characterized by warmth, concern for the college, and devotion to its religious principles. According to statements made by students . . . they place a high value on the friendliness of the faculty and their readiness to respond to personal requests for help, whether in studies or personal problems.

For Rocket, one of the technical-vocational colleges, the report is quite different:

The order of the day seemed to be a kind of standardized urban anonymity. Serious-faced young men came and went singly, in pairs, or in small groups, chatting pleasantly and easily in quiet tones. Beyond the immediate circle, however, the other students were treated as strangers with the not unfriendly distance often accorded other people eating in a restaurant or traveling on a train. A number of faculty complained of the lethargy of the students saying, "They seem to have no interests. They are commuters and their lives are lived away from the college. They come to class, take notes, and go away."

At Kildew and Classic, the liberal and experimental colleges, friendly and informal relationships were relatively frequent and a strong sense of cummunity was reported. Kildew students and faculty operated for the most part on a first name basis. Each student had a faculty counselor, usually of his own choice, and it was expected that individual conferences would be held every one or two weeks. In this context, as well as in the small classes, in independent studies, and in numerous student-faculty committees, close relationships of mutual regard developed. The sense of community seemed to be particularly strong at Classic, although few persons could define precisely what it meant to be a Classic type. As at Kildew, this sense of community derived from a wide range of informal, inexplicit, and frequently unidentified agreements and understandings learned through living as a member of the college community.

The curricula also differed from group to group. The conservative colleges' programs conformed quite closely to the standard undergraduate liberal arts curriculum. The organization of course requirements, the content of courses, and the procedures for evaluation were in harmony with those which would be found in most college catalogs. Distribution requirements assured that each student would take at least one or two courses in the humanities, natural sciences, and social sciences, course content was predictable, and students were evaluated by quizzes, midterms, finals, and papers.

The curricular offerings at technical-vocational colleges differed primarily in their emphasis on business, engineering, and applied technologies. The general studies component was emphasized, but still, a student's program was determined heavily by his particular area of vocational concern. Thus the technical-vocational colleges differ primarily in the content of their curricula, since their procedures for teaching and evaluation were similar to the traditional methods employed by the conservative colleges.

Classic and Kildew differed from the other Project colleges and from each other. Classic had a highly structured and tightly integrated curriculum, emphasizing skills in analysis, rhetoric, logic, and integration, with the aim of providing a comprehensive background of basic information. Classes were usually intense , small group discussions of carefully selected reading materials, often prepared in mimeographed form by the faculty members responsible for a particular course or sequence. Students were evaluated through comprehensive examinations in the humanities, natural sciences, and social sciences, and by "integrative" examinations in foreign languages, history, and philosophy.

Kildew's student-centered and highly flexible curriculum contrasted vividly with Classic. There were no required courses. Independent study was open to all students from the second year onward. Students were expected to undertake three studies each semester but they could carry only two if the nature of their studies warranted that. They could pursue independent study singly or with one or more students who shared similar interests and who could agree on a plan of work for the semester that a teacher would approve. Courses arose out of the interests of the students and the interests and capabilities of the teachers. The usual system of examinations and grades was replaced by a system of written self-evaluations and instructor comments, and the last four or five days of each semester were given to conferences between students and their teachers about the work of the team.

It is interesting, however, that the Kildew and Classic approaches, while contrasting sharply with one another, both produced high levels of intellectual interest and social concern. In neither case was there a major emphasis on scholarship in the usual sense of the word. At Classic the emphasis aimed at developing one's own competence and analytic skills through intense examination of ideas and concepts. At Kildew the emphasis aimed more directly at building on one's own purposes and interests to produce greater clarity and productivity in response to personal and social concerns.

The pictures of these three different groups of colleges that emerge from the CUES scales, the on-campus visits, and other data not reported here are highly consistent. Institutional objectives, college programs and practices, and other characteristics of the colleges fit together in coherent fashion, and the institutions within each group are much more similar with each other than with the institutions in the other groups.

As might be expected, these institutions, and the other Project Colleges as well, attracted and admitted very different student personalities. The emphasis on formal religion and on practical achievements in the church-related colleges is accompanied by identical correspondence in religious conservatism and practical outlook on the part of entrants. At church-related colleges where commitment to Christian principles and living by them is primary, impulses are carefully controlled, new ideas are treated cautiously, and altruism is important. These freshmen also are interested in practical applied activities and tend to value material possessions and concrete accomplishments. They are authoritarian and conservative, and are not very intellectually oriented. They are inclined to deny interests in aesthetic matters and to evaluate ideas on the basis of their immediate practical application.

At the liberal-experimental colleges, Kildew and Classic, which emphasize awareness of self and of society, entrants are more ready to accept feelings and to express them, and they also show altruistic concern for others. These freshmen show diverse interests in the arts, as they appreciate literature, music, and dramatics. They enjoy reflective thought and academic activities and their thinking is relatively free from domination by objective conditions and generally accepted ideas. They also are usually analytical, logical, and critical in their approach to problems. They admit to being sensitive and emotional.

At the professional-vocational colleges, Rocket and Stonewall, where vocational preparation and personal achievement is emphasized, altruism is least evident among the entrants. Emotional expression is tempered, the risks of innovation are seldom taken, and their orientation toward practical achievement is accompanied by more limited concern for the feelings and welfare of others than was the case for entrants at the church-related and liberal-experimental colleges.

Do the characteristics of the dropouts differ from group to group, or do the generalizations described in Chapters 2 and 3 continue to be apparent among these very different institutions? The answer to this basic question turns out to be both yes and no.

In some characteristics, differences between leavers and stayers were consistent for all three groups. Dropouts were more impulsive, more responsive to their own feelings and emotions. They shared a more complex view of things, were more tolerant of ambiguity, more open-mind-ed. They were more autonomous and less likely to give the socially desirable, expected answers designed to make a good impression.

In other characteristics, however, the leavers differed from group to group. At the conservative church-related colleges, most students who stayed subscribed to the community spirit and conformed to the model student explicitly set forth by the college. They did what was expected of them, behaved properly, and questioned themselves and society much less than the students who withdrew. Those who withdrew were more anxious and less well-integrated. They were less altruistic and more liberal—religiously and socially. The climate of the college supported the personal organization of those who stayed. It was consistent with their high altruism and their conservative religious beliefs. The campus climate provoked less anxiety for them than for those who left.

Students who withdrew from the technical-vocational colleges were more interested in ideas and intellectual matters and less concerned about practical achievement. In addition to being more impulsive, complex, and independent, they were less authoritarian, less anti-intellectual, and more interested in science and scientific activities than their classmates who stayed.

Students who withdrew from the liberal and experimental colleges showed high levels of anxiety and strong esthetic and artistic interests. They were even less concerned about practical achievements and success than their classmates who stayed, even though everyone's general concern for achievement was minimal.

The basic principle which these findings clearly document is that whether a student becomes a dropout depends not only on the particular background and personal characteristics he brings with him to college, but also on the characteristics of the institution he meets when he arrives. Although generalizations do distinguish dropouts and transfers from each other and from those who stay, those general characteristics operate with different force in varying college environments. Clear understanding and helpful responses, therefore, require not only that the personal characteristics of dropouts be understood, but also that the relationships between those characteristics and the forces generated by different institutions be clearly identified.

This basic principle is powerfully driven home by the findings which emerged when the differences between leavers and stayers were examined more thoroughly for all the Project Colleges. Table 6.2 presents these differences for the scales of the Omnibus Personality Inventory on which dropouts were most different from those who stayed.

The striking thing about these results is the high frequency with which the distinguishing characteristics of dropouts within the colleges persisted across the wide range of various institutions and despite the wide range of individual differences among students at entrance. On the Impulse Expression (IE) scale, for example, in every case (men and women separately for seven colleges, business and engineering students separately for one), dropouts scored higher than stayers. In seven of these cases the differences were statistically significant. Most important, they were higher regardless of the average institutional scores at entrance. At W.J.B., for example, where students scored substantially below the national average at entrance, both men and women dropouts had significantly higher scores (52 versus 46 and 46 versus 38, respectively). At Kildew, where entering students generally score almost at the top of the scale, both men and women dropouts had higher scores than their persisting peers (66 versus 63 and 60 versus 58 , respectively). On the Complexity (Co) scale, Sacred men and women dropouts scored 48 versus 46 and 46 versus 44, while at Classic the scores were 61 versus 58 and 63 versus 60. This pattern is repeated time after time on these scales. In every case where there are statistically significant differences the pattern of within college differences holds regardless of score level.

The pervasiveness of this pattern means that it is not the absolute level of impulse expression, complexity, autonomy, practical outlook, and personal integration that is important. Instead, it is the position of a student in relation to his classmates that determines whether he leaves or stays (cf. Nasatir, 1963). Compared with other college students across the country, the dropouts from the church-related colleges are cautious, conservative, conforming, and dependent. But compared with their peers who continued in those colleges, they are impulsive, complex, autonomous, creative. At the other end of the spectrum, stayers at the two liberal-experimental colleges are highly creative, impulsive, complex, and autonomous, yet the students who left scored still higher, pushing the top of various scales as they searched for an institution where their own needs and purposes could be more adequately met.

These observations and the more detailed findings which underlie them illustrate a fundamental point further supported by data from other studies examining the interaction of student and college, for example, Gurin, Newcomb, and Cope (1968). Just as each institution attracts a particular kind of student, it also repels and retains its own brand. Some students find each college satisfying and valuable, others do not. Satisfaction, however, depends not only on the college and its program, but also on the tastes and tolerances students bring at entrance— and these differ. For example, Rocket leavers come with steady dates and a group of friends; Divinity leavers do not. Divinity leavers bring little experience in extracurricular activities; Stonewall leavers bring

TABLE 6.2 DIFFERENCES BETWEEN DROPOUTS (DO) AND STAYINS (SI) WITHIN EIGHT COLLEGES ON THE OMNIBUS PERSONALITY INVENTORY (MEAN SCORES)*

	Number of Students		Impulse Expression (IE)		Complexity (Co)		Autonomy (Au)		Religious Liberalism (RL)		Practical Outlook (PO)		Personal Integration (PI)		Anxiety Level (AL)	
	DO	SI	DO	SI	DO	SI	DO	SI	DO	SI	DO	SI	DO	SI	DO	SI
W.J.B.																
Men	21	25	52	46	48	45	44	44	39	38	56	54	50	53	48	51
Women	26	26	46	38	46	43	44	39	40	36	54	55	48	55	49	53
Savior																
Men	31	32	48	46	47	44	40	43	40	42	58	57	50	50	48	50
Women	42	41	44	38	43	43	41	40	40	39	58	58	46	51	46	48
Sacred																
Men	23	15	54	52	48	46	42	40	46	44	57	58	46	49	47	47
Women	51	46	47	45	46	44	43	41	43	41	55	56	49	51	49	50
Divinity																
Men	26	50	48	45	48	46	49	45	40	39	49	53	54	55	52	54
Women	60	47	42	41	44	44	46	45	38	38	52	52	53	53	51	51
Kildew																
Men	25	45	66	63	64	64	62	62	60	60	41	41	44	48	41	47
Women	39	47	60	58	65	62	66	62	63	62	37	40	48	48	47	46

Classic

Men	65	59	60	57	61	58	61	60	60	58	41	44	50	51	48	50
Women	47	30	59	57	63	60	61	59	58	55	39	41	45	48	43	47

Stonewall

Men	283	241	57	56	49	48	44	44	50	49	56	57	47	47	47	46
Women	86	89	52	48	48	46	42	41	48	45	56	57	46	46	45	46

Rocket

Business—																
Men	31	72	60	55	50	46	47	45	51	48	55	56	51	50	50	48
Engineer—																
Men	43	53	58	51	50	48	48	44	51	49	54	56	49	51	49	52

*Underlined scores indicate statistically significant differences ($p < .05$). Appendix H includes a brief description of selected Omnibus Personality Inventory Scales.

more such experience than do those who stay. Stonewall leavers were hard workers in high school; Divinity leavers were not. Leavers chose Rocket because of its entrance requirements and convenient location; they chose Divinity because of its values and ideals. These sharp differences and the unique patterns which result mean that the small college cannot rely solely on findings from generalized research conducted elsewhere. Each institution must look carefully at those characteristics which distinguish its own leavers and then act accordingly. Divinity, Stonewall, and Rocket each must develop quite different approaches to the problem of attrition, and the program developed by one is not likely to suit another.

At some colleges the problem is still more complex. At Stonewall, for example, there are important differences between the men and women leavers: social class differences, differences in high school background and experience, differences in relationships with parents. At other Project colleges important sex differences also occurred. Behold, men and women are different! Obvious? Indeed. But coeducational liberal arts colleges have yet to recognize significant differences when they exist, and to manage admissions, curriculum, or counseling accordingly. These findings concerning student attrition add to the evidence that such discriminating action is called for.

At some colleges the characteristics of leavers vary depending on the program or department with which they are associated. Research at large universities has demonstrated this, and the differences between engineering and business leavers at Rocket are another example. Engineers come more frequently seeking academic and intellectual development and challenge; they bring more wide-ranging interests. The business leavers come for vocational preparation as intellectual development is not so important. The kinds of program modification that would reduce attrition among the engineers might well have opposite consequences for business students. Thus when a college has quite distinct programs that draw persons of different backgrounds and inclinations, then separate studies of attrition and differential modifications may be required within each program, rather than for the whole institution. The next chapter suggests how colleges may go about studying and improving their programs to enhance retention or to enhance healthy withdrawal to other more challenging and fruitful environments.

CHAPTER SEVEN

PROMISING COLLEGE PRACTICES: THREE CASES

Colleges want to initiate programs to reduce attrition but are faced with the problem of not knowing which areas of student life should be improved, since records are incomplete and every college is different.

It is possible to piece together an inventory of program-related reasons for attrition if a number of facts are pulled together. From the registrar's office, requests for transcripts before and after departure tell something about which institutions are attracting the leavers. It is possible to estimate the number who had to leave for reasons of poor health by examining health records. With help from the financial aids officer, it is possible to estimate the number who left simply because they could not afford to remain. From the counseling office, an estimate of the number and nature of personal problems leading to withdrawal can be calculated. The office of student affairs will have information on the number of students asked to leave for disciplinary reasons, the dean's office will identify academic dismissals, and the business office may have some information on students withdrawing from the residence halls. It is possible, but extremely unlikely, that such information could be pieced together to provide a meaningful overall picture of reasons for withdrawal.

The best source of useful information may be the student who left. It is equally important, however, to know how students in similar situations persist. A simple survey of both continuing and withdrawn students that asks them to identify problem areas is a useful device, as the following examples illustrate.

A CHURCH-RELATED COLLEGE

One small, church-related college in the Southeast discovered, despite years of encouraging and continuous growth, what they considered a serious problem with retention. When the director of institutional research looked beyond total enrollment, he discovered that 25 to 40 percent of the college's total student body withdrew each year; furthermore, in most years only 25 percent of the entering freshmen graduated with their class (see Tables 7.1 and 7.2). A survey of both continuing and withdrawn students was conducted using a questionnaire such as the one illustrated on page 93. This survey provided answers to questions such as: Was the college's remote location causing students to withdraw? Were increasing costs driving students away? Was the curriculum meeting the student's needs?

After comparing the problem areas of both continuing and withdrawn students, the college learned that the location was perceived as a significant problem, cost was a problem, and the curriculum—at least from the perspective of women—was somewhat narrow. These problems, however, were comparable for all students; that is, they were not less significant for the persister. One surprising discovery was that approximately one in every three entrants had not planned to complete degree requirements at the college anyway, and thus dropping out or transferring had been, for them, a planned outcome. They usually transferred to colleges where they could enter an occupational specialty that the college could not offer (e.g., nursing) or they came to the college for a special purpose that was not related to their long-range plans (Bible courses). Over 50 percent of the women had no intention of graduating when they enrolled! That college is now beginning to examine

TABLE 7.1   NUMBER AND PERCENTAGE OF ENTERING FRESHMEN GRADUATING WITH THEIR CLASS AT A SOUTHEASTERN, CHURCH-RELATED, LIBERAL ARTS COLLEGE

Year of Entrance	Number of Original Entering Freshmen	Number Graduating with Their Class	Percentage of Original Class at Graduation
Fall 1965 (Class of 1969)	97	18	18.5
Fall 1966 (Class of 1970)	96	25	26.0
Fall 1967 (Class of 1971)	114	28	24.5
Fall 1968 (Class of 1972)	111	45	40.5
Fall 1969 (Class of 1973)	110	30	27.3
Fall 1970 (Class of 1974)	125	36	28.0

TABLE 7.2   ATTRITION PER YEAR BY CLASS AT A SOUTHEASTERN, CHURCH-RELATED, LIBERAL ARTS COLLEGE

	1966–1967	1967–1968	1968–1969	1969–1970	1970–1971	1971–1972	1972–1973	1973–1974
Enrollment	250	307	299	328	354	378	454	447
Attrition								
Freshman to Sophomore	30	58	39	46	57	64	76	46
Sophomore to Junior	26	38	26	34	43	55	43	50
Junior to Senior	19	19	12	19	17	29	21	18
Total annual attrition	75	115	77	99	117	148	140	114
Annual attrition rate	30%	37.5%	25.8%	30.2%	33.1%	39.2%	31.1%	25.5%
College-year attrition rate	N/A	N/A	9.7%	10.7%	10.5%	10.1%	N/A	N/A
Summer attrition rate	N/A	N/A	16.1%	19.5%	22.6%	29.1%	N/A	N/A

how its program will provide maximum benefits to both the degree-oriented and the nondegree-oriented student, and how recruiting can attract *even more* students who find the college's less-than-degree-oriented programs attractive for short terms.

In sum, the college, despite the apparently startling dropout statistics, did not find there was a particular problem that they could remedy. Twenty-five percent of the students graduated on schedule, an additional 15 percent graduated later, and 33 percent did not have plans to graduate; this accounted for 73 percent of the students. The information from the remaining 27 percent of the former students suggested a variety of reasons for withdrawing, none of which appeared significant enough to require any special programming. Better counseling, more financial aid, relaxed rules, miscellaneous curricular modifications, higher standards for admission, marriage, and a host of other largely unrelated needs were mentioned. When the students were asked, "What, if anything, could the college have done to assist you in remaining at the college that was not done?" Over half the respondents answered "nothing," or left the space blank; the others gave equal mention to an expanded curriculum (10 percent) and more financial aid (10 percent) and last mention to the need to relax rules (5 percent) and to provide better counseling (5 percent). In short there was no need for concerted action in particular areas. The college did, however, recommend a series of steps to improve the college program as a whole, giving each department rather specific responsibilities. This college also requested administrator and faculty input during the "dropout" study and requested suggestions from the staff on how to implement a program based on the study's findings. Recommendations for each department followed, along with specific suggestions from interested staff. The college's action report is given in Table 7.3.

Table 7.3 RECOMMENDATIONS BY DEPARTMENT

For Administration

The President must take the leadership/initiative in establishing greater cohesion among various components of the college constituency (trustees/administration/faculty/staff/students and donors.) Specifically, not just designate office hours when President is available but set aside time for seeking out informally groups of students and/or faculty and openly share college's problems but listen also to their concerns.

For Academic Office and Faculty

1. Promote and encourage more faculty contact with students outside class-

---

room experience. This would include social and cultural activities, athletic events, and hospitality in faculty homes.

2. Urge faculty to not only teach the theory of their disciplines but also seek to demonstrate how these theories would work out in practice, i.e., through field trips or actual participation in some related activity.

3. Seriously evaluate academic costs, examine trends (both at the College as well as nationally), and determine student needs re majors, and be ready to adjust curriculum and program within the liberal arts framework.

At least three students have left the College and have transferred to other colleges this summer because of our Psychology Department. Over the past 6–7 years the teaching staff in the Psychology Department has not increased at all. As a result the course offerings have been limited.

Our social science program needs real strengthening. For instance Warren M., in his recruiting, indicated a real desire on the part of many students to major in sociology.

In short a study should be made to determine where the demand for courses lies and to bolster those departments accordingly. It also means that some subject areas might be deemphasized.

Jack M.

One of the best ideas the college could develop is to build a reputation in training excellence in two or three vocational subject areas, while at the same time maintaining a strong liberal arts program. If the college were widely known for its programs in such areas as journalism, business ed., or church music, a large number of students would be attracted. I feel that the college will have to do something more in vocational areas, but it would be a mistake to try to branch out into a dozen or so areas, each one a small department.

Craig P.

I would recommend either the institution of a Department of Business Administration or an arrangement with the University of Georgia or U.T.C. for a preprofessional course in business.

R. G. A.

Develop ways of using Chattanooga as a learning laboratory—"environmental" education.

Jack F.

Hire a Christian economist to give leadership in the area of economic principles for students wishing to go into the business area.

Hire another man in the area of sociology-psychology for a major in the area of social service.

Lou V.

4. To make college somewhat more practical in the perception of the students, list or show the kind of courses that may be used for preprofessional or vocational programs.

   Each department should brainstorm on programs that could be "assembled" using the sources already available. Example: Create a program leading to Director of Christian Education by having Education and Bible courses combined.

   Create and advertise a lot of preprofessional courses such as prelaw, premedical, etc. Most of these programs require core courses anyhow.

   Get together with U.T.C. to combine programs such as special education, early childhood, business administration.

   Jack F.

5. Create rap sessions on earthy and controversial issues.

6. Raise academic standards while consciously helping weak students to learn study habits so that eventually we will attract better students because of our scholarly reputation. (See item 2 under Admissions.)

   Work harder at promoting student initiative academically. It may carry over more into independent dorm discussions. We tend to paternalistically "give answers" too easily. As faculty we have to stop thinking of ourselves as "teachers of courses" and more as scholars seeking mastery of a discipline. It may carry over to the student level.

7. We need more live discussion among the faculty on interdisciplinary questions and Christian perspective. If faculty are not discussing problems, neither will the students.

For Student Development Office

1. Counseling/Advising

   a. Identify students who plan to stay for only one or two years and those who are uncertain and assist them in understanding the value of liberal arts Christian education.

   b. Offer workshops for students to develop proper study habits and the stewardship of time. Faculty advisors should be used, with a good resource person developing and presenting the program.

      There needs to be more counseling of students in terms of their goals, I believe. Faculty need some help in this area—it shouldn't be assumed that a faculty member in a particular discipline would be aware of all the possible career goals associated with his discipline. The Student Affairs Office, perhaps, could help the faculty in this counseling.

      C. W. D.

   c. Establish better communications between student Affairs Office and faculty advisors regarding status or problems with advisees.

4. Seek to make dorm conditions more conducive to study by encouraging (not legislating) quiet evenings and plenty of sleep at nights (so students will be more alert in class).

5. Seek to encourage and promote cultural activities in the city and arrange transportation for such.

6. Arrange for regular transportation service to city and shopping centers on a regular basis during the week.

7. Urge athletic coaching staff to inculcate not only a rightful pride in sportsmanship but also genuine humility in interpersonal relations with other students (vs. the snobbishness that some students have perceived).

For Business and Development Office

1. Study ways and means to assist worthy students to finance their education with scholarships and loans. We must keep in mind that Federal grants and loans are being more widely distributed and geared to lower income families, leaving middle class people in a difficult position to finance a college education.

2. Complete the Prayer Room Project, including furnishings.

Admissions

1. Seek to maintain high standards for entering students.

2. Introduce a college prep program designed for special and probationary students. Perhaps we should reconsider the compensation education program for disadvantaged students.

3. Since nationally, students tend to enroll in colleges within 200 miles, and since the continuing Southern Presbyterian Church has no college, I recommend that a new college recruiter be hired to concentrate in the south and southeastern U.S.

    Much student attrition seems to come because of the College being too far away from their homes. I recommend a greater concentration of student recruitment in the Greater Chattanooga area.

    R. G. A.

Chapels

1. Have more small chapels—not just with faculty as leaders, use perhaps some senior students also—but be sure these are well-planned in advance.

2. Have assembly programs where deans or other administrative spokesmen realize the rationale for our philosophy of Christian Education and rules and regulations of the College.

    August 1973

A PRIVATE LIBERAL ARTS COLLEGE

A private liberal arts college in southern Illinois with comparable rates of attrition found, unlike the church-related college, that the results from a follow-up survey did suggest particular problem areas that the college could do something about. The college asked *three* groups of students to respond to evaluative statements about the college and about themselves: presently enrolled, withdrawn, and graduates. The results indicated that improvements in several areas would enhance retention—the most striking in the area of advising and counseling. Every mention of advising or counseling, such as career guidance, help with personal problems, and academic program advice, was considered an important problem to the respondents and they suggested that the services were inadequate and that more was expected, particularly among the students who had withdrawn. Those who had graduated gave the lowest rating to the advising services, suggesting that improvements were already taking place; but they called particular attention to the need for an improved placement service, since nearly half indicated career counseling and placement services were clearly inadequate.

The atmosphere in the residence halls was identified as another problem, especially among those who had departed. The physical facilities and the social environment were satisfactory, but the conditions for study were singled out for low evaluations with comments about too much noise.

Responses from those who transferred suggested the college should carefully consider offering majors in special education and business, since many moved to concentrate in those areas. A substantial proportion of the transferring students also felt the course work was not challenging; so, if the college was erring on standards, it was not on the side of being too difficult.

While some areas for improvement were singled out, the general reaction indicated that students were generally satisfed with the college and were in fact pleased with its faculty, curriculum, facilities, and location. The written responses were especially complimentary to the faculty. The faculty and administration's concerns about financial aid, the quality of teaching, and the semi-rural location were not endorsed by the students.

As a result of this study, the college launched what it called a "Student Alert System." Within the first year, these results were reported: Before we did the attrition study, we were losing approximately fifty per cent of the students who were undecided about their majors. Now that we have started counseling with those students, we lost only twenty-three per cent. . . . Our freshman attrition went from approximately forty per cent to twenty-five per cent. . . . We are currently working out a major in Special Education with a nearby state university to help the Special Education problem.[1] The details of the Student Alert System are given in Table 7.4.

Table 7.4   STUDENT ALERT SYSTEM

The primary goal of this system is to reduce attrition. Reduced attrition means increased revenue. Increased revenue is very important with the financial situation as it is in most colleges and universities today. More important is the fact that reducing attrition saves students from dropping out of college needlessly.

After an extensive attrition study, we found that a high percentage of those leaving were either undecided about their major or had changed majors two or three times. Another concentration of students leaving seemed to be those who had self-doubts about the value of a college education. This same group tended to be slightly dissatisfied with various areas of our institution. However, this dissatisfaction tended to say to us that a group of our students who were leaving, normally the "silent attrition," had various individual problems.

It was this discovery that led us to ask ourselves "How can we identify these students at an early time so as to solve some of their problems and save them from becoming attrition?" We also asked ourselves "What are the symptoms of a student getting ready to leave college?"

We identified several points which indicated a student may become dissatisfied with college. It was around these points that we built our "Student Alert System."

Undecided Major

One major point of which we immediately became concerned was that of the undecided majors. These persons were identified from the registration information and contacted by the Registrar to offer her services in helping them select a major course of study. This decision is made only when the time is right for that individual to select a major. I must stress that no student is forced to select a major. We only let the student know that we understand this often difficult decision and offer our help or services when possible. We offer several interest inventories to assist in this decision.

Frequent or Excessive Change of Major

A record is kept of each student as to his major for a given term. If the record indicates that any student's major has changed more than twice, the Registrar makes contact with the student to discuss the situation. Again this must be conducted in a low-keyed, nonthreatening manner.

---

[1]Personal correspondence with the Director of Institutional Research.

Request for Transcripts to Other Colleges

Any time a student who is not graduating requests a transcript to be sent to another college, the Registrar interviews that student. The intent of the interview is to be sure there is nothing we can do to allow that student to continue at the College. Occasionally, we find minor problems by this process which can be resolved, and often cause the student to change his mind about transferring.

Students not Preregistered

Any student who does not preregister for the following semester is immediately identified and contacted to see if that student intends to return the following term. The list of students not intending to enroll are turned over to the Student Affairs Office to determine the reason. This follow-up at an early date allows any student who has minor resolvable problems time to enroll if he desires.

Freshmen and Transfer Student Interviews

The Student Affairs Office interviews all freshmen and transfer students after about the fourth week of classes during the Fall Term. The purpose of this interview is to let that student know we are genuinely interested in him and his problems and to identify problems students are having at an early time to keep them from growing worse with time.

Students Not Signed Up for a Room for the Following Term

These students are followed up by the Student Affairs Office to determine if they are returning at an early date so as to identify any problems.

Students Failure to File for Financial Aid

The Financial Aids Officer plays a key role in following up on those who fail to file for financial aid to determine who does not intend to return the following term. These students are contacted by the Student Affairs Office to determine the reasons. Again the key is to do this process early to allow time for enrollment if the student is interested.

Faculty Role

The faculty notify the Student Affairs Office when a student suddenly stops attending class, grades suddenly drop, or shows unexplainable disinterest. These are symptoms of the student having some kind of problem. The Student Affairs Office follows-up on these students to see if any solution can be worked out. If the problem turns out to be academic, an interview is set with the Vice President for Academic Affairs for the student.

Student Employment Supervisors

If a student quits work or suddenly becomes disinterested in his work the Student Affairs Office is notified. If the supervisor does not know the real reason for quitting, the Student Affairs Office attempts to find out so as to help the student solve the problem.

Business Office

If a student is unexplainably late in paying a bill, the Student Affairs Office is notified. The student is contacted to determine the problem.

Residence Hall Staff

The Residence Hall Staff are on the alert for any problems which may be leading to attrition. Many problems with students seem to be more readily identified at midterm and the end of the term, especially academic problems of which the student is not making grades to his expectation.

Student Alert Record

Each of the preceding problem areas are reported to the Student Affairs Office. A card is kept on each student reported. This makes a good reference for future problems. It also allows for an accurate study of the reasons for those students who finally leave.

It must be understood that we are not pressuring any student into doing something against his will. We are only making a genuine attempt to give that individual student the care and concern he deserves. In the process, our attrition figures are getting smaller each term.

There are some reasons for attrition we will never solve: marriage, transfer because we do not offer the major, family problems, personal problems, health problems, etc. We will only be able to better predict the amount of students who will fall into these categories. Again, some valuable infomation for predicting enrollments and knowing how many students have to be recruited in order to have a certain size enrollment.

ALERT SYSTEM

DATE _____

STUDENT'S NAME_____

INFORMATION FROM_____

CONCERN _____

_____

_____

Return to Student Affairs Office or call Extension 31 or Extension 38.

A PRIVATE UNIVERSITY

A private university in Florida used still another variation of the technique of follow-up studies. They decided to devise a questionnaire containing items relating to satisfaction–dissatisfaction in 34 areas of student life, which would also contain a question concerning the student's plans to return or not to return to the university during the following session; thus, attrition was defined as the students' *plans* to leave rather than the actual fact of leaving in a past semester. Results comparing persisters and nonreturners indicated that the area of dissatisfaction most highly correlated with attrition was the student's sense of not making progress toward academic and career goals. They did not find any of the student services, life in residence halls, or finances related to attrition.

Twice as many nonreturning students were dissatisfied with their progress toward both their academic and career goals as those returning; the same proportion of students expressed dissatisfaction with the quality of instruction and out-of-class contact with the faculty. These were the four clearest differences between the returning and nonreturning students—all academic. In fact, 12 of the 17 items (out of 34) correlated with not returning to college were in the academic area. The word faculty appeared in four items and each of these items was related to attrition: the quality of instruction, freedom felt to contact faculty for consultation, availability of faculty for consultation, and faculty involvement outside the classroom. The obvious suggestion for this institution was that the faculty would be its key to improved retention.

However, an area of high dissatisfaction is not necessarily related to attrition, whereas an area of low dissatisfaction might be. For example, 81 percent of the students were dissatisfied with the sensitivity of the administration to student needs, yet dissatisfaction in this area was not correlated with attrition. Conversely, only 24 percent of the students were dissatisfied with progress toward their academic goals, yet this dissatisfaction had the highest correlation with attrition.

These examples illustrate the point we make throughout: colleges are different and each college must examine how it may improve its own program, given its unique academic offerings, location, type of student, student mix, competing institutions, financial position, staff, history, and purposes. Students, too, are infinitely variable. An approach to the problem that might prove effective, however, is described below.

First, in order to see if withdrawals might be a problem, collate data such as those in Tables 7.1 and 7.2. If a problem is present, go to the students and have them evaluate the experiences they and only they know well. The type of questionnaire illustrated in Table 7.5 is a useful

TABLE 7.5   THE WASHINGTON STUDENT SURVEY

Please Note

In this questionnaire you are asked what you are doing now, and what kinds of problems you experienced at the University. This survey depends on the sincerity and frankness with which you answer the questions. Your cooperation, the vital factor in the success of the study, is greatly appreciated.

Start Here

1. What are you doing at the present time? (Please be specific for example: "I am a fulltime student at the University of Washington majoring in political science," or "I am married and working while my husband attends Oregon State University," etc.)

I am a missionary for the Church of Jesus Christ

of Latter-Day Saints (Mormon) working in

Indiana and Michigan for two years.

2. If you are no longer at the University of Washington please give your reason or reasons for leaving. (For example: "I couldn't find other students who shared my interests so I enrolled at Reed College after my freshman year," or "My grades were disappointing so I transferred to Western Washington College," etc.)

I have left to fulfill this mission and plan to

return to the U of W after November 1971 to

continue my E.E. studies.

3. Below is a list of some experiences and situations which students have often named as having troubled them during their years at college. You may have encountered some of these situations at the University of Washington. For each situation consider *how much of a problem* it was or has been for you at the *University of Washington*. Please circle ONE alternative for EACH statement.

	Crucially important to me	Very important to me	Fairly important to me	Not too important to me	Not at all important to me
A difficulty developing proper study habits— utilizing my time	4	3	(2)	1	0
A fear of academic failure—not able to maintain a "C" average	4	3	(2)	1	0
A disappointment in a relationship with the opposite sex—a hurt, loss, or rejection	4	3	2	1	(0)
A feeling of being lost at the University because it is so big and impersonal	4	3	2	(1)	0
A concern that my religious beliefs were being challenged and threatened	4	3	2	1	(0)
A problem with the police or with the disciplinary agents of the University	4	3	2	1	(0)
A disappointment in having too little contact with the faculty	4	3	(2)	1	0
An inability to find individuals or groups with whom I could identify	4	3	2	(1)	0

device when modified to reflect the circumstances at a particular institution (for example, see Appendix F).[1] The responses to such a questionnaire will help in the construction of an evaluative graph such as that illustrated in Figure 7.1. The wide part of each bar shows the range within which about two-thirds of the students expressed problems; the thin line extends from the first to the ninth decile (90 percent of the cases); and the cross line represents the average response. The selected problem areas in this graph are, in fact, drawn from a study at a large

	Crucially important to me	Very important to me	Fairly important to me	Not too important to me	Not at all important to me
Disillusionment with the purpose of a college education	4	3	2	(1)	0
A disappointment with the "snobbishness" of most social groups on campus	4	3	2	1	(0)
The failure of the coursework to challenge me intellectually	4	3	2	(1)	0
Impatience with the superficiality of much that is considered a part of college	4	3	(2)	1	0
A feeling that the University is not active enough in promoting needed changes in our society	4	3	2	1	(0)

The foregoing list is by no means intended to exhaust the set of problems encountered by students. Therefore you are invited and encouraged to elaborate some concerns which stand out as important in your experience at the University. (Use extra sheets if necessary.)

Thank you for participating in this study.

[1]Under the direction of Walter Schoen (1974), Educational Testing Service has developed an evaluative questionnaire for students that assesses a wide range of college services including instruction, counseling, administrative regulations, class scheduling, student activities, faculty contact, the library, the bookstore, and more. If a college does not decide to use the prepared booklets and scoring sheets, the items are instructive and may be adapted to a particular college's setting. The original intent of the Student Reactions to College Project was to develop an evaluative instrument specifically for the community college, and the items are thus most appropriate in that context; but a version is also available from Educational Testing Service for the four-year college. The questionnaire is also designed for students in residence, but could be adapted to the requirements of a study of leavers.

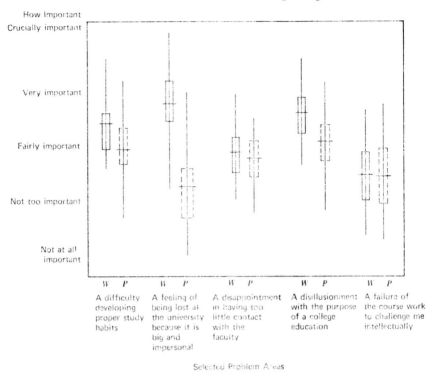

Figure 7.1 Comparing withdrawn students with persisters on problems encountered while in attendance: conceptual schematic.

public university in the West which compared responses of continuing and withdrawn students. These data suggest, first, that study habits are about equally important to the two groups (note the overlapping responses). Second, the size of the institution is experienced as a significant problem by those who had withdrawn; but perception of size as a problem seems unrelated to amount of faculty contact since a disappointment in contact with the faculty is equally shared between the two groups. Reading the questionnaires clarified what "big" and "impersonal" mean to the students; they usually referred to the social environment, getting to know people, having friends who cared, getting to know members of the opposite sex, and so on. The third inference made is about the meaning of a college education both to the continuing student and to the person who left. Many of the students who left seemed to be asking themselves, "Why college?" Finally, the challenge of the course work did not *seem* to separate the continuing and departed student.

Data like these, of course, provide a starting point for self-study. But additional analysis refines first impressions. Figure 7.2 is based upon these same data but has separate profiles for four groups of students: (1)

Figure 7.2 Comparison of withdrawals with persisters on importance of problems encountered while at the university. W_{AC} = academic withdrawals; W_{IC} = intellective-cosmopolitan withdrawals; P = persisters; W_{SOC} = social withdrawals. The number of cases is given in parentheses.

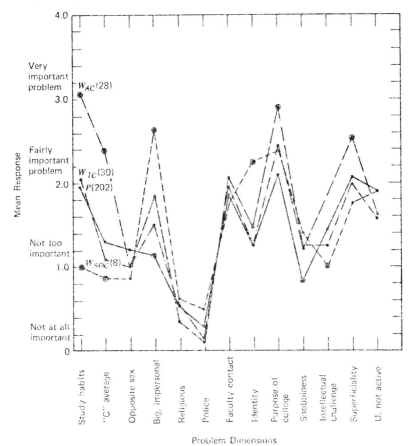

academic withdrawals—students who failed in their studies or were having great difficulty meeting the academic standards; (2) social withdrawals—students who seemed overwhelmed by the social atmosphere, were not accepted, could not make friends, but who were not in academic difficulty; (3) intellective-cosmopolitan—students who left because they found the intellectual and social climate "stifling" or not "intellectually challenging"—these are polar opposites from the academic and social dropouts; and (4) a sample of persisting students.

These additional data (all mean scores) suggest that subgroups of students may have problems that are masked by larger grouping: study habits are of great importance to those who fail (as expected), but least important to those whose goals are social; the size of the campus is important to all the withdrawn students, but particularly important to the social withdrawee; doubts about the purpose of a college education are more important to withdrawn students, but are most important to the most able intellective-cosmopolitans, as is their concern for the superficiality of college, and lack of intellectual challenge in the course work.

A NOTE ON FOLLOW-UP TECHNIQUES

Obtaining a reasonable response rate is often a problem in follow-ups. Basically, the questionnaire must be short and simple, the appeal honest and attractive. Also, the process should be personalized by use of first-class mail rather than bulk rates, stamps rather than a meter, personally signed cover letter and follow-up letters even if they are printed or autotyped. In addition to personalizing the process, the importance of every response should be stressed and the respondents should be offered a summary of the findings. Mailings should be timed to arrive at homes when they might be expected to be visiting parents (holidays). And reminders should include a complete questionnaire rather than be simply a postal card reminder. Two or three follow-up mailings must be anticipated if returns are to exceed 60 to 70 percent.

Can one rely on response from students who are no longer at the college? We find the respondents are candid, more candid than if they are asked questions while still in attendance; and since they are no longer under the control of the college, they see things in a better perspective, and are usually anxious to help.

In one of our follow-up surveys, for example, we felt the quality of the response was particularly good. The evidence supporting this judgment is based on several factors. First, the high response rate (nearly 80 percent) suggested "motivated" respondents. In addition, many personal letters (about 30) were received from the respondents who wanted to say more than the questionnaire permitted in sections allotted for comments. A substantial number of responses were returned air mail from overseas without benefit of the business reply envelope—not a small extra expense to the respondent. Above all, the respondents were, as we suggested above, candid. For example, to the question, "Why did you withdraw from the University?" we received responses such as the following: "I got married, my grades were unsatisfactory, and I was pregnant—but not necessarily in that order;" "I had a nervous breakdown;" "A married teaching fellow with several children was trying to date me, so I thought it better to go to another college;" "I left to have an abortion . . . however, I plan to return next year;" "I was busted for pot and I'm serving a short sentence in the clanger;" and so on.

What do we know about nonrespondents? The nonrespondents are undoubtedly the most dissatisfied of all students—dissatisfied with society and the college. It is relatively easy to obtain the candid responses such as the foregoing from students who, while having problems, do not relate those directly to the policies and practices of the institution. The hardcore nonrespondent tends to be either the student who is completely alienated and finds the questionnaire one more intrusion into one's personal life or the student who was so burned by the experience at the school that it borders on hate. In either case the questionnaire ends in the wastebasket, and probably in shreds. We know about these students because of efforts to contact them via telephone. They *are* candid on the phone about why they will not fill out the questionnaire: "I reject any such intrusions into my life and thoughts," and "I hate the place so much . . ." are typical. Even if they will agree to fill out the questionnaire if another is sent, do not expect to get it back. They *are* hard core. Any follow-up study with a large nonresponse rate cannot rely on the evaluations made solely by the respondents.

While we recommend using a questionnaire that allows the student to give a narrative response, we do not want to over simplify the problems of interpretation. An example of a response which was difficult to interpret is this reply from a student who left a large university to transfer to a university of similar size:

If I may take this opportunity without being accused of excess verbiage let me say that in my case the fault lay not with the University which is a fine institution (and I have the advantage of comparison) but with my own half-formed and impotent character. The time of development when one goes to college is crucial in that one simply has to become a person without the crutch of the family image; no one can do a great deal to aid this process but the one involved and I am sure it would have occurred in my own slow case. The size of the institution is certainly of some importance but I can assure you that Michigan is a 'place' and has a strong atmosphere of closeness; one identifies with the institution and its intimacy. Imagine a school of comparable, even larger, size whose physical limits were as vacuous as its subjective confines, where one never encountered the same face, where one had the feeling of attending a large city—imagine and be comforted.

CHAPTER EIGHT

SUMMARY AND RECOMMENDATIONS

Before suggesting guidelines for action, we summarize our main findings which, like our recommendations, are simple and straightforward:

ABOUT RATES OF DROPPING OUT, WHO DROPS OUT, AND FROM WHAT KINDS OF INSTITUTIONS

- The withdrawal rate is high, has been high for the 50 years of attrition research, and seems to change little over time. Between 40 and 50 percent of the entering students earn baccalaureate degrees in four years, 20 to 30 percent graduate later, and the remaining 30 to 40 percent never earn degrees. (See pages 1–5).
- Since most talented students persist in their studies toward degrees, there is little attrition among the most promising entrants, at least in terms of degrees earned. (See pages 30, 60–61).
- Men and women discontinue, stopout, transfer, and so on in approximately equal proportions, but for different reasons: men more often because of matters related to competence, adequacy, and identity searching; women more often because of intellectual-aesthetic and social dimensions, including dating and marriage. (See pages 13–16, 61).
- Colleges know little about the reasons for withdrawal, the process of withdrawal, or the actual proportion of students leaving their campus. (See pages 5–6, 81).
- The rate of college degree completion varies considerably among different colleges and universities. The prestigious private universities experience little attrition over four years, while some of the less prestigious private colleges, the state colleges, and the community colleges

have most of their students withdraw prior to completion of any degree. (See pages 60–61).

• The primary factor in "holding power" is the student's identification with the college. Colleges are more likely to retain the student who chooses the institution because of its clear image values and program, and knows this is what he or she wants. (See pages 20, 32–33, 75–80).

WHY STUDENTS WITHDRAW

• Most quantitative research (such as admissions data) is without value in either predicting withdrawal or understanding the reasons for discontinuance, since such research considers a limited number of variables, usually easily quantified, such as high school grade point averages, college entrance test scores, parents' income, socioeconomic class background, participation in high school activities, and the like. In addition, the reasons for discontinuance are usually complex, overlapping, often have nothing to do with the student, and in some instances may not even be recognized by the student. Changed vocational choice, poor choice of the college in the first place, meeting a loved one and transferring to be with him or her, dissatisfaction with the college, fulfilling less than degree expectation, and other multifaceted issues are involved in withdrawal. (See pages 31–45).

• It seems clear too, that there is no dropout personality, only individual personalities interacting with different campus environments, at various times in their mutual and changing lives. (See pages 38–45).

WHAT HAPPENS TO THE DROPOUT

• The positive results of discontinuance (permanent or temporary) are often so substantial that there may be good reasons to encourage even more students to at least stop out, if not drop out. (See pages 59–67).

Our major conclusion is that dropping out is not a problem in its own right, but rather a symptom of other conditions. Our basic premise is that the conditions associated with what we have described as the dropout problem will be alleviated when students are free to learn in new ways, in different settings, and in varying time periods. Most of the recommendations that follow are based on this premise and the view of higher education's historical legacy which follows.

For nearly three centuries American higher education followed a system inherited from England in which every student took the prescribed curriculum which was taught in a similar sequence with the same group in four years. Some changes were introduced around the turn of the century (e.g., electives), the curriculum was expanded, and we have moved toward mass higher education; but the current practices in colleges and universities are largely based on the premise that students are there full time for four years. Obviously, full time for four years is far from true today and will be even less true by the turn of this century when learners will be freer to learn in ways, settings, and time periods more suited to their individual needs.

Within higher education there are clear signs that we are recognizing the new realities, yet in the prospective student's view, even today, there are the stereotypes built on that old model: the four-year college as a citadel of learning, an instrument of rational thought, a place of commitment, integrity, and reason, dedicated to human growth and the improvement of society. Most freshmen still bring to college a naive and boundless idealism concerning the ways of higher education. Even though they think they know how a particular school differs from others, nevertheless, the particular pattern of courses, requirements, individual student personalities, attitudes of faculty and administrators, and what we have called the environmental presses usually come as a surprise. Few colleges fulfill a student's initial expectations and thus most students are soon disillusioned, some seek their idealized model elsewhere, most adapt and stick it out.

Unfortunately, the sources of information on what college is like (friends, family and high school counselors) share the common stereotype, which is reinforced by the college catalog and the perceptions of college administrators.[1] They are not likely to change or become more insightful, for parents remember selected features of college as it was, counselors tend to be products of a particular type of education and have a limited sense of what other schools are really like, and few peers have been to college. As a result, freshmen will continue to be disillusioned by the discrepancies. Given this inevitable disillusionment, colleges should be prepared either to assist students to transfer or to help them adapt to the more realistic (if cynical) view of the typical upperclassman.

---

[1]Only one other group on most campuses has been found to share the freshman myth—college administrators. "Evidently, both read the same literature!"—the college catalog (Stern, 1970, p. 176).

RECOMMENDATIONS

ADMISSIONS AND EXIT PROCEDURES

• Colleges must make it easier to enter and exit, at least facilitating, if not encouraging, stopping out. While the American system is already more flexible than others, consider the implications of this view from a colleague in Britain:[2]

On the question of dropping out, one of the things that I am concerned about in Britain is that it is so difficult to drop out! For a variety of reasons—for example, the stigma of dropping out, the difficulty of transferring grants, the difficulty of finding alternative university places—students tend to carry on with their courses even though they may find out fairly quickly that they have made a mistake. By and large most of the people who leave British Universities without completing their degrees have failed, or failed to take some examination or other. Hence, if you leave university before time, people—including employers—tend to assume you are an academic failure. This position has been exacerbated by the introduction of numerous resit examinations so that a smaller proportion of students are now being asked to leave the university as a result of poor exam performance and, hence, those that are, are regarded as bigger failures. Thus it takes a very brave student to withdraw voluntarily because he does not like the course; and this sometimes results in the rather wasteful situation of someone struggling on for four years with a course in, say, chemical engineering and finding with some relief at the end of it that he is acceptable as an income tax inspector!

• Colleges must move farther away from the concept of the two-year or four-year degree; they should encourage intermittent or interruptible schooling and lessen requirements for continuous registration, thus making it easier for students to take a leave of absence. Even in colleges where leaves of absence are permitted, we find few students realize it is easy to obtain an official leave of absence, thus making it easier to return.

• Self-selection is a key factor of success in college. The values of an individual related to the particular institutional values are one of the primary determinants of persistence. This relationship points out the need for institutions to clarify these values in the minds of entering students and to examine the admissions procedures for possible adjustment.

• The model of selective admissions based on test scores and grades

[2]Personal correspondence from Alan Smithers, Senior Lecturer in Education, University of Bradford, November 1974.

is inappropriate. Colleges should place more admissions emphasis on "whole-person" indicators of accomplishment (creative writing, a hobby in science, a goal in life, etc.). These students are much more likely to become outstanding individuals than those with high scores on SATs and ACTs, which offer virtually no indication of capacity for significant intellectual or aesthetic contribution in later years (Wallach, 1972).

ALTERNATIVE ROADS TO AN EDUCATION

• The large pool of noncompleters is likely to be attracted to external degree, Extended University, Open University, University Without Walls, and other concepts, and this development should be encouraged.

• Colleges should arrange for drop-ins to avail themselves of campus resources without the usual hassle of getting admitted to the college and accepted by a department. Residence halls can be used to accommodate transient students, especially in urban areas, where a student may only be on a campus for a brief period to take a workshop or some other brief learning experience.

• In keeping with the concept of encouraging educational opportunity for all ages and people in all circumstances, in addition to various open university concepts, it may be possible for more colleges to experiment with more academic calendar options (e.g., 4–1–4) or Friday-Saturday Colleges.[3]

CREDIT

• Colleges should increase the awarding of credit for knowledge and experience formerly unaccreditable, and thus move toward competence or achievement-oriented degrees.

• Colleges should eliminate arbitrary designations such as sophomore, junior, and senior; instead, students should accumulate credits as indicators of progress toward degrees.

• Potential stopouts might be encouraged to remain with the college if credit could be awarded for approved independent study and experi-

[3]Mount St. Mary College, Newburgh, N.Y., has recently established a Friday-Saturday program in which it is possible to be awarded a baccalaureate degree in four years. "It seems to meet the dropout's expectations and needs ideally, but it is a bit too early to evaluate" (personal correspondence).

ence off-campus, particularly when the project is student suggested and self-directed and the student is seeking "real world" experience.

LIFELONG LEARNING

• Since students who have withdrawn have already shown a willingness for higher education, they form an immense pool of potential students; we know that those who already have the most learning are most likely to engage in further learning.

• External credit and noncredit options should be made available to leavers as well as a wider audience.

• Colleges should allow credit for life's experience, especially for those who started, but had not finished college.

• Colleges should recognize credits earned many years ago; the arbitrary "no-credit-for-credits-earned-over-ten-years-ago" provision at most colleges is simply that—arbitrary.

In essence, we are saying that in a world of rapidly changing technology, with its emphasis on continuing education and periodic retraining, there is less and less reason to maintain boundaries between college and college, school and society, school and work, student and nonstudent. Lessening the emphasis on the prescribed full-time and four-year status provisions in college and university practice will be a positive step toward new patterns of lifetime education in which individuals can choose for themselves from among multioption educational lifestyles.

THE PART-TIME STUDENT

• To encourage part-time study, colleges should alter the tuition structure which penalizes the part-time student in about half the colleges and universities.

• Colleges should provide more financial aid to the part-time attender.

• Basic opportunity grants from the federal government should not require full-time or full-year study.

• Social security benefits should be available to the part-time student just as there should be tax deductions for study part time.

RESEARCH

The aspect of follow-up study which has the greatest potential value involves testing the development of leavers and their peers who stay on to graduation. With the data thus generated, leavers who transfer, stopout, or who go to work, and students who stay on to graduate can be compared with each other. Through such comparison, the relative contributions to student development of the college first attended, of the colleges to which students transfer, and of working experiences can be assessed. Such information will enable more sound judgment about the impact of college in general and about the impact of particular kinds of colleges, matters of major importance to the participating colleges, to others like them, and to higher education in general. More important for the problem of attrition, such information will enable better judgments concerning the developmental consequences that follow from leaving the college of initial entry. This is the ultimate basis on which distinctions between productive and nonproductive withdrawal can be made, the ultimate basis on which action concerning student attrition must rest.

TRANSFERRING STUDENT

• Colleges must recognize that transferring students have about the same problems of finance and adjustment as typical freshman, and the disparity between aid available to freshmen and transfers should be changed. In particular, we call attention to the financial aid that might be made available to transfer students from community colleges; many able community college students may not be continuing their education simply because financial help gets targeted at freshmen.

• Community colleges too may assist in the transfer process by recognizing a "retreading" role. The number of transfers from community colleges to four-year colleges is recognized. Not noticed is the *larger* number of transferees that often flow from the university and four-year colleges *to* community colleges, especially in urban areas. Community colleges help many university students "recover" and return to a baccalaureate degree program.

• Small colleges need to take another look at their policies for granting credit for courses taken at other institutions, ". . . transfers take a credit beating at small institutions; they are twice as likely to lose a semester there as are students with comparable grades transferring to large institutions" (Willingham and Findikyan, 1969).

• The passport, a new type of student file under development by Educational Testing Service and scheduled for application in 1975, deserves support. A 4-by-6-inch microfiche containing nearly 100 pages of student-constructed information, including high school and college grades and recommendations is intended to replace the traditional application form. Progress by transportable passport may become important.

A CONCLUDING THOUGHT

Many and varied experimentations with the college experience have met with limited success, while the demise of some programs are well-publicized in newspapers and academic journals. Such efforts are often meant to counter criticism from both in and out of the world of academia; and some efforts are specifically designed to meet the problem of student attrition. Unlike the turtle who, when startled, withdraws and reassesses, it seems to us that institutions of higher learning are like the hare who bounds along without aim or goal simply to escape what is perceived as impending disaster. It is a self-protective or self-maintaining phenomenon; institutional reaction is often far removed from thought of what is best for, or needed by, those who are being served. In essence, colleges do not know the market and, by trial and error, often attempt to reawaken interest with untried methods designed for an inadequately researched clientele. What research is done is segmented; conclusions and inferences are drawn from limited data and produce much dialogue, but rarely solutions. Even in attrition research, the common and best predictors—GPA, SAT scores, and so on—do not predict and provide little help in solving the problem of withdrawal from college.

We suspect that fighting a tide or current is hardly productive in terms of survival. Strong river currents, irresistible ocean tides, or howling blizzards cannot be fought when one is in their center. Such natural circumstances can be borne, understood, and overcome only with conscious assessment of their danger, and with attitudes toward them which provide for survival. Such times are not for trial and error—the error may exert a cost beyond the capacities of some to pay.

What is the tide or current in higher education today? Most educators know. It seems mainly to be a question of value. Students are asking if a college education is really necessary. Consistently, they have been told to question, and so they do. They even question the basic premises of a college experience. It seems that the "chicken has come home to roost." Those who taught students to question are themselves being questioned and their institutions are being questioned along with them. But the sources of college attrition do not stop there. The problem is multifaceted. Leaving college may rest in a multitude of reasons when large proportions of freshman classes leave every year. Can an institution sort out so many variables and hope to make the number of adjustments necessary to correct the programs and environment for all? Probably not. To fight such a current or tide may be like "blowing in the wind." Since it seems hopeless, should we give up? We think not. But like the turtle, the institution must reassess and must change its attitude concerning reality perhaps by going with the current or tide, by seeking to help its clients rather than trying to "assure" its own survival. For, in going with those it is meant to serve, colleges may tend to increase their chances of healthful survival and avoid expending energies in fruitless directions.

But what does it mean " to go with the tide"? It means simply, as this book has tried to suggest, that to fight student withdrawal is analogous to working against survival. As the old saying goes, "To help others is to help oneself." Thus a different attitude is needed, various roles must be learned, more adequate rules must be developed, a new understanding of what education is—formal and informal—should be created. Life is for learning and all of life is included. Therefore, the uninterrupted four-year sequence for all students should become a thing of the past.

Regarding attitudes, it is perhaps too often said that professors are purveyors of information. But something too often said is not often heard. The professor must become aware of whether he or she considers himself or herself to be master of resource. Perhaps the latter is the more commendable position in terms of the students' self-learning process. It is also often said that dropping out is to be discouraged, and professors perhaps foster that attitude more often than not. If a professor's attitude is one of helpfulness, his response to a student's desire to leave college for a time should be affirmative, allowing the student to make the decision and suggesting alternatives, but never pressing. If education continues throughout life, then the professor's attitude should be one of recognition that learning during a stopping-out period falls within, and is congruent with, a lifelong educational process. Such attitudes may well bring the student back as a returnee later on. Thus a positive approach to the student may result in a by-product of institutional survival.

But what about roles? The foregoing paragraph has described the professor as a resource person rather than as a master, an advisor rather than a director. The difficulty of changing teachers' roles is evident in educational research. Where new ideas have been tried, success has not been guaranteed because of the "Law of Driftback." Even though faculty may wish to change their roles, it is much easier to drift back to traditional roles because they are more comfortable. This is where the institution's responsibility enters. It cannot expect the professor to accept new roles without new training. Faculty development is primarily an institutional responsibility and not a natural phenomenon occurring during a faculty member's career. Thus the role of the institution must change to become less an instrument of administration and more an academic planning and training institute for faculty by training its own members to carry on a more efficient and effective academic community committed to student self-learning. Included in this change of roles is a change in role of the student to that of a self-starting, self-directed learner. This can be developed in students only if a reorientation to learning is begun in the students' first year through encouragement of individual program development, individual research, and independent study.

Institutions receive much criticism because of the rules and requirements imposed on admissions and in awarding of credit for students' past achievement. Most credit awarded at entrance depends on the requirements of the specific institution with regard to majors. According to most admitting institutions, transferable credit must come from recognized institutions and must parallel the courses prescribed in given areas. As a result, students lose credit and money paid for such experiences and much discouragement results. If courses are passed satisfactorily at one institution, they should be accredited and accepted by another. For, if all learning and all experience gained in the higher learning is education (i.e., in the context of new attitudes), then successful learning should be valuable enough to count toward a degree— or, more important, toward an educated person. All educated men and women are strong in some things and weaker in others and absolute balancing within individuals is rarely achieved. The institution's decision to accept some credits and not others is almost always arbitrary. The reduction of this unnecessary frustration and loss would go far in lowering student attrition.

In conclusion, attitudes, roles, and rules in higher education need modification if the symptom of dropping out is to be lessened. And, if such changes do occur, it is possible that fewer reports on attrition will occur or be needed in the future, since leaving college will have become part of the learning process. Leaving college will be a necessary action for some students as a part of on-going lifelong learning. The college door will be one that revolves freely to allow an entrance and an exit for students at appropriate times—to reassess, to lower tension, to get married, to relax, to play on the one hand; and to return, to think, to study, to learn on the other. As one man of wisdom said, "time is used for different purposes":

A time to plant, a time to pluck up . . .
A time to get, a time to lose;

A time to keep, and a time to cast away . . .
A time to keep silence, and a time to speak. . . .[4]

In other words, students of all ages operate in unprescribed zones, times, and seasons; everything has its own season, faster for some, slower for others. Such an approach provides for the *variousness* in all individuals.

[4]Ecclesiastes 3:2–7.

REFERENCES FOR FURTHER RESEARCH

AND APPLICATION[1]

Abel, W. H. 1966. "Attrition and the Student Who Is Certain." *Personnel and Guidance Journal*, **44**(10):1024–1045.

Aiken, J. 1968. "A Comparison of Junior College Withdrawees." *EDO23389*.

Aiken, L. R. 1964. "The Prediction of Academic Success and Early Attrition by Means of a Multiple Choice Biographical Inventory." *American Educational Research Journal*, **2**:127–135.

Alfert, E. 1966. "Housing Selection, Need, Satisfaction and Dropout from College." *Psychological Reports*, **19**(1):183.

Alfred, R. 1972. "1971–72 Student Attrition: Antecedent and Consequent Factors." *EDO70435*.

Alfred, R. 1973. *Student Attrition: Strategies for Action*, Community College Conference Proceedings. Kansas City: Metropolitan Junior College District, May 9–10, 1973.

Altman, R. 1959. "The Effect of Rank in Class and Size of High School on the Academic Achievement of Central Michigan College Seniors, Class of 1957." *Journal of Educational Research*, **52**:307–309.

Ammons, R. M. 1971. "Academic Persistence of Some Students at St. Petersburg Junior College." *EDO63929*.

Anderson, B. C. 1967. "Comparison of enrolled and Non-Enrolled Applicants for Modesto Junior College, Fall 1966." *EDO14303*.

Astin, A. 1964. "Personal and Environmental Factors Associated with College Dropouts among High Aptitude Students." *Journal of Educational Psychology*, **55**:219–227.

Astin, A. 1971. *Predicting Academic Performance in College*. New York: Free Press.

Astin, A. 1972. *College Dropouts: A National Profile*. Washington, D.C.: American Council on Education.

Astin, A. 1973. "Research-based decision making in Higher Education: Possibility or Pipe Dream?" Paper presented at the meeting of the Higher Education Colloquium, Chicago.

Astin, A. 1973. "The Impact of Dormitory Living on Students." *Educational Record*, **54** (Summer):204–210.

[1]The ERIC references (identified by the prefix "ED" and a number at the end of each citation) were obtained from an ongoing extensive bibliographic compilation by Irene Shrier and David Lavin (1974). We gratefully acknowledge their work and commend it to others.

Astin, A. 1975. *Preventing Students From Dropping Out*. San Francisco: Jossey-Bass, Inc.

Astin, A. and Panos, R. 1968. "Attrition Among College Students." *American Educational Research Journal*, January:57–72.

Astin, A. et al. 1967. "National Norms for Entering College Freshmen, Fall, 1966." *ACE Research Reports*, **2**(3).

Astin, A. et al. 1974. *The American Freshmen: National Norms for Fall 1973*. Los Angeles: Cooperative Institutional Research Program, UCLA.

Astin, H. S. 1970. *Educational Progress of Disadvantaged Students*. Washington, D.C.: Human Service Press, University Research Corporation.

Athey, I. J. and Trent, J. W. 1966. "Student Characteristics Associated with Varying College Attending Pattern." *EDO3060*.

Augustine, R. D. 1966. "Persistence and Attrition of Engineering Students, A Study of Freshman and Sophomore Engineering Students at Three Midwestern Universities." *EDO14740*.

Axmaker, L. W. 1970. "The Effect of Group Counseling on the Self-Concept, On the Motivation to Achieve, and On the Proportion of Dropouts Among Unselected Community College Students at Southwestern Oregon Community College." *Dissertation Abstracts International*, **30**(10–A):4214.

Bachman, G. et al. 1971. *Dropping Out—Problem or Symptom?* Ann Arbor: Institute for Social Research.

Bard, B. 1969. "College Students: Why They Drop Out." *The Education Digest*, **34**(March):18–21.

Barger, B. and Hall, E. 1964a. "Personality Patterns and Achievement in College." *Educational and Psychological Measurement*, **24**(2):339–346.

Barger, B. and Hall, E. 1964b. "A Report on Exit Interviews Conducted by the Offices of the Deans of Men and Women: Students Withdrawing During the Winter Trimester." University of Florida, Mental Health Project Bulletin No. 13, (July).

Barger, B. and Hall, E. 1965. "Interaction of Ability Levels and Socioeconomic Variables in the Prediction of College Dropouts and Grade Achievement." *Educational and Psychological Measurement*, **25**(2):501–508.

Barger, B. and Hall, E. 1965. "Time of Dropout as a Variable in the Study of College Attrition." *College and University*, **40**(1):84–88.

Baxter, C. W. 1968. "Relationships Between Organizational Variables and Student Withdrawal Rates in Junior Colleges." *Dissertation Abstracts*, **28**(10–A):3914–3915.

Bayer, A.E. 1968. "College Dropout; Factors Affecting Senior College Completion." *Sociology of Education*, **41**(3):305–316.

Bayer, A. et al. 1973. *Four Years After College*. ACE Research Report 8. Washington, D. C.: American Council on Education.

Beahan, L. T. 1966. "Initial Psychiatric Interviews and the Dropout Rate of College Students." *The Journal of the American College Health Association*, **14**(April):305–308.

Beals, E. W. 1973. *College Transfer Students in Massachusetts*. Boston: Board of Higher Education.

Bean, A. 1971. "Personality Measures as Multiple Moderators in the Prediction of College Student Attrition." *Dissertation Abstracts International* **32**(1–A):229.

Beaver, D. P. 1973. "A Cluster Program for High Risk College Students." *College Student Journal*, **7**(April–May):61–65.

Beford, F. L. 1967. "The Dropout—Salvation of American Education." *Arizona Teacher,* **55**:5–6

Bemis, J. F. 1962. "A Study of Undergraduate Students Who Voluntarily Withdrew from the University of Washington." Doctoral dissertation, University of Washington.

Berg, I. 1970. *Education and Jobs: The Great Training Robbery.* New York: Praeger.

Berls, R. 1969. "Higher Education Opportunity and Achievement in the United States." *The Economics and Financing of Higher Education in the United States.* Washington, D. C.: Joint Economic Committee, Congress of the United States.

Beyer, D. E. 1972. "An Analysis of Selected Intellectual and Non-Intellectual Characteristics of Dropouts and Survivors in a Private College." *Dissertation Abstracts International,***32**(7–A):3773.

Bisconti, A. and Astin, H. 1973. *Undergraduate and Graduate Study in Scientific Fields.* Washington, D.C.: American Council on Education, Research Report No. 8.

Black, D.B. 1972. "Farewell, Drop-Out: Hello, Drop-in." *Stoa,* 31–37.

Blai, B., Jr. 1970. "'Success' of 'Calculated Risk' Students at Harcum Jr. College." *EDO40699.*

Blai, B., Jr. 1971. "First to Second Year Student Attrition Among Junior Colleges." *Scientia Paedagogica Experimentalis,* **8**(1):8–15.

Blai, B., Jr. 1972. "Two Year College Dropouts—Why Do They Leave?" *EDO58879.*

Blanchfield, W. C. 1971. "College Dropout Identification: A Case Study." *Journal of Experimental Education,* **40**(2):1–4.

Blanchfield, W. C. 1971. "College Dropout Identification: A Case Study, Utica College." *EDO58605.*

Bogue, E. 1969. "A Factor Study of Biographical Characteristics Associated with Nonpersisting Freshmen Students." *Dissertation Abstracts,* **29**(9–A):2914.

Bossen, D. 1968. "A Follow-up Study of the Junior College Withdrawal Student." *Dissertation Abstracts,* **29**(5–A):1418.

Bossen, D. A. and Burnett, C. W. 1970. "What Happens to the Withdrawal Student?" *Junior College Journal,* **40**(9):30–32.

Bowman, D. L. 1970. "Reducing Freshman Attrition and Preparing Teachers for the Disadvantaged." *EDO51112.*

Bowman, D. and Campbell, L. 1971. "Attack on High Attrition of University Under-Achievers." *Journal of Teacher Education,* **22**(2):210–214.

Boyer, E. L. and Michael, W. B. 1965. "Outcomes of College; Early Withdrawal from College." *Review of Educational Research,* **35**(4):277–279.

Bragg, E. A. 1956. "A Study of Student Withdrawal at 'W.U.'" *Journal of Educational Psychology,* **47**(April):199–202.

Brown, F. G. 1960. "Identifying College Dropouts with Minnesota Counseling Inventory." *Personnel and Guidance Journal,* **39**:280–282.

Brown, T. 1969. "The Urban University Student: Selected Factors Related to Continuation and Withdrawal." *Dissertation Abstracts,* **29**(12–A):4318.

Brown, W. E. et al. 1971. "Effectiveness of Student-to-Student Counseling in the Academic Adjustment of Potential College Dropouts." *Journal of Educational Psychology,* **62**(4):285–289.

Bucklin, R. W. and Bucklin, M. 1970. "The Psychological Characteristics of the College Persister and Leaver. A Review." *EDO49709.*

Bureau of University Research. 1967. "Study of Dropouts by Majors of New Freshmen and Undergraduate Transfers Entering September 1962, February and September 1963, February and September 1964, February and September 1965, February 1966 with Academic Standing at Time of Last Attendance." (Mimeograph), Northern Illinois University, March.

Campbell, A. and Eckerman, W. C. 1964. *Public Concepts of the Values and Costs of Higher Education.* Ann Arbor: Survey Research Center.

Capper, V. L. 1969. "The Effects of Two Types of Reinforcement on Dropouts, Class Attendance, and Class Achievement in a Junior College, Continuing-Education Mathematics Program." *Dissertation Abstracts International,* **30**(6–A):2413–2414.

Carlson, S. J. and Wegner, K. W. 1965. "College Dropouts", *Phi Delta Kappan,* **46**(March):325–327.

Center for Research and Development in Higher Education. 1967. "On Creativity." *The Research Reporter,* University of California, Berkeley, **22**:1–4.

Centra, J. and Rick, D. 1971. "College Environments and Student Achievement." *American Educational Research Journal,* **8**:623–634.

Cervantes, L. F. and Husted, G. P. 1970. *Dropout: Causes and Cures.* Review in *Personnel and Guidance Journal,* May.

Chambers, J. L. et al. 1965. "Need Patterns and Abilities of College Dropouts." *Educational and Psychological Measurement,* Summer **25**(2):509–516.

Chase, C. I. 1965. "The University Freshman Dropout." *Indiana Studies in Prediction, No. 6.* Bureau of Educational Studies and Testing, Indiana University.

Chase, C. I. 1970. "College Dropout: His High School Prologues; Indiana University." *National Association of Secondary School Principals Bulletin,* **54**(342):66–71.

Chickering, A. W. 1966. "Institutional Differences and Student Characteristics." *Journal of Amerson College Health Association,* December:168–181.

Chickering, A. W. 1969. *Education and Identity.* San Francisco: Jossey-Bass.

Chickering, A. W. 1974. *Commuting Versus Resident Students.* San Francisco: Jossey-Bass.

Chickering, A. W. and Hannah, W. 1969. "Process of Withdrawal." *Liberal Education,* **55**(December):551–558.

Chickering, A. W. et al. 1968. *Research and Action.* Third Annual Progress Report. Washington D.C.: Council for the Advancement of Small Colleges.

Clark, B. 1960. "The 'Cooling-Out' Function in Higher Education." *American Journal of Sociology,* **64**:569–576.

Cliff, N. 1962. "An Investigation of the Factors Associated with Dropout and Transfer by Scholarship Applicants." (Research Bulletin RB-62-13). Princeton, N.J.: Educational Testing Service.

Cohen, M. 1969. "The Relationship Among Student Characteristics, Changed Instructional Practices and Student Attrition in Junior College. Final Report." *EDO32074.*

Cohen, M. and Brawer, B. 1970. "Student Characteristics; Personality and Dropout Propensity." *EDO38130.*

Cohen, M. et al. 1969. "Selected Personality Correlates of Junior College Dropouts and Persisters." *EDO27883.*

Coker, D. L. 1968. "Diversity of Intellective and Non-Intellective Characteristics Between Persisting and Non-Persisting Students Among Campuses, Wisconsin State University." *EDO33645.*

References

Colberg, D. 1971. "Why Students Fail; A Student Symposium." *Library College Journal*, 4(1):26–57.

"College Applicants, Entrants, Dropouts." 1965. *U. S. Office of Education Publication.* United States, Office of Education (OE-54034).

"College Dropout and Talent Utilization; Conference at Princeton University." 1965. *School and Society*, 93(March 6).

College Entrance Examination Board. 1973. *A Survey of the Admission, Enrollment and Retention of Black Students at Predominantly White Colleges in the South.* Project Opportunity Report No. 2, CEEB Southern Regional Office.

Congdon, J. D. 1964. "Personality Factors and Capacity to Meet Curriculum Demands." *Personnel and Guidance Journal*, 42:17–31.

Conner, J. D. 1968. "Relationship Between College Environmental Press and Freshman Attrition at Southern Methodist University." *College and University*, 43(3):265–273.

Cope, R. G. 1966. "Economic Variables and the Prediction of College Attendance and Achievement." *College and University*, 41(1):35–40.

Cope, R. G. 1967. *Differential Characteristics of Entering Freshmen Environmental Presses and Attrition at a Liberal Arts College.* Unpublished doctoral dissertation, University of Michigan.

Cope, R. G. 1968a. "Academic Performance in Higher Education: A Review and Critique of the Literature." (Draft), Office of Institutional Studies, University of Massachusetts, December.

Cope, R. G. 1968b. "Limitations of Attrition Rates and Causes Given for Dropping Out of College." *Journal of College Student Personnel*, November:386–392.

Cope, R. G. 1968c. "Selected Omnibus Personality Inventory Scales and Their Relationship to a College's Attrition." *Educational and Psychological Measurement*, 28:599–603.

Cope, R. G. 1969a. "College Press and Dropouts." *EDO28467.*

Cope, R. G. 1969b. "Types of High Ability Dropouts Who Continue in College." *North Central Association of Quarterly*, 44(2):253–256.

Cope, R. G. 1970. "Sex-Related Factors and Attrition Among College Women." *Journal of the Association of Women Deans and Counselors*, 33(3):118–124.

Cope, R. G. 1972. "Are Students More Likely to Drop Out of Large Colleges?" *College Student Journal*, 6(2):92–97.

Cope, R. G. and Hewitt, R. G. 1971. "Types of College Dropouts: An Environmental Press Approach." *College Student Journal*, 5(September–October): 46–51.

Cope, R. G. et al. 1971. "An Investigation of Entrance Characteristics Related to Types of College Dropouts. Final Report." *EDO52749.*

Creager, J. A. et al. 1969. "National Norms for Entering College Freshmen Fall 1969." *ACE Research Report*, 4(7).

Cullen, J. B. 1973. "Social Identity and Motivation." *Psychological Reports*, 33:338.

Cummings, E. C. 1949. "Causes of Student Withdrawals at DePauw University." *School and Society*, 70:152–153.

Dalrymple, W. 1967. "College Dropout Phenomenon; Facts, Theories and Programs." *NEA Journal*, 56(April):11–13.

Daniel, K. B. 1963. "A Study of Dropouts at the University of Alabama with Respect to Certain Academic and Personality Variables." Doctoral dissertation, University of Alabama.

Daniel, K. B. 1967. "Study of College Dropouts with Respect to Academic and Personality Variables." *Journal of Educational Research,* **61**(January):230–235.

Davis, B. H. 1970. "The Community Junior College Experience as Perceived by Students Who Have Withdrawn." *ED046386.*

Davis, H. 1971. "Incidence and Type of Psychiatric Disturbance in Dropouts from a State University," *Journal of the American College Health Association,* **49**(4):241–246.

Davis, J. A. 1966. "The Campus as a Frog Pond." *American Journal of Sociology,* **72**:17–31.

Demos, G.D. 1968. "Analysis of College Dropouts: Some Manifest and Covert Reasons." *Personnel and Guidance Journal,* **46**:681–684. Also *ED014735.*

DeVecchio, R. C. 1972. "Characteristics of Nonreturning Community College Freshmen." *Journal of College Student Personnel,* **32**(5):429–432.

DiCesare, A. C. et al. 1970. "Non-Intellectual Correlates of Black Student Attrition." *ED049714.*

Drasgow, J. and McKenzie, J. 1958. "College Transcripts, Graduation, and the MMPI." *Journal of Counseling Psychology,* **42**:125–128.

Dresser, D. L. 1972. "The Relationship Between Personality Needs, College Expectations, Environmental Press and Undergraduate Attrition in a University College of Liberal Arts." *Dissertation Abstracts Inter.,* **32**(9–A):4979.

Dryhand, D. 1969. "Expectations Concerning the College Experience as They Relate to the Academic Achievement and Persistence of Freshmen." *Dissertation Abstracts International,* **32**(6–A):2373.

Dutt, L. 1972. "Student Persistence in College. An Analysis." *Dissertation Abstracts International,* **32** (9–A):4943.

Dyer, H. 1968. "School Factors and Equal Educational Opportunity." *Harvard Educational Review,* **37**:38–56.

Dysinger, W. S. and Hackman, J. R. 1966. "Attrition in the Liberal Arts College." *ED010622.*

Eagle, N. 1973. "Dropout Prediction at an Urban Community College Following Open Admissions." Paper read at the American Educational Research Association, New Orleans, February.

Eckland, B. K. 1964a. "A Source of Error in College Attrition Studies." *Sociology of Education,* **38**(1):60–72.

Eckland, B. K. 1964b. "College Dropouts Who Came Back." *Harvard Educational Review,* **34**(3):402–420.

Eckland, B. K. 1964c. "Social Class and College Graduation: Some Misconceptions Corrected." *American Journal of Sociology,* **70**:60–72.

Elias, E. M. and Lindsay, C. A. 1968. "The Role of Intellective Variables in Achievement and Attrition of Associate Degree Students at the York Campus for the Years 1959–1963." *ED030406.*

Ellis, V. 1967. "Students Who Seek Psychiatric Help." In J. Katz, (Ed.), *Growth and Constraint in College Students: A Study of the Varieties of Psychological Development.* Stanford, Calif.: Institute for the Study of Human Problems, Stanford University.

Elton, C. and Rose, H. 1971. "A Longitudinal Study of the Vocationally Undecided Male Student." *Journal of Vocational Behavior,* **1**:85–92.

Escher, F. 1973. "Retention-Attrition Report." St. Joseph, Minn.: College of St. Benedict.

"Failed to Stay Course." 1967. *Times Education Supplement,* November 3.

Farine, A. 1973. "Demographic and Social Accounting: A Follow-Up on the Withdrawals from Quebec Colleges." Paper read at the American Educational Research Association, New Orleans, February.

Farnsworth, D. S. 1955. "Some Non-Academic Causes of Success and Failure in College Students." *College Admissions,* 2:72–78.

Farnsworth, D. S. 1947. *Mental Health in Colleges and Universities.* Cambridge: Harvard University Press.

Faunce, P. S. 1966. "Personality Characteristics and Vocational Interests Related to the College Persistence of Academically Gifted Women." Doctoral dissertation, University of Minnesota.

Faunce, P. S. 1968. "Personality Characteristics and Vocational Interests Related to the College Persistence of Academically Gifted Women." *Journal of Counseling Psychology,* 15(1):31.

Fenske, R. H. and Scott, C.S. 1973. *The Changing Profile of College Students.* American Association for Higher Education, Research Report No. 10.

Fenstemacher, W. 1973. "College Dropouts: Theories and Research Findings." In R. Cope, (Ed.), *Tomorrow's Imperatives Today.* Seattle: Association for Institutional Research.

Fleisch, S. and Carson, E. R. 1968. "Boston University Class of 1970 Dropout Rate." Interim Report No. 1. Boston, Mass.: Boston University.

Folger, J. K. et al. 1970. *Human Resources and Higher Education.* New York: Russell Sage.

Foote, N. N. 1951. "Identification As the Basis for a Theory of Motivation." *American Sociological Review,* 16:14–21.

Ford, D. H. and Urban, H. B. 1965. "College Dropouts; Success or Failures?" *Educational Record,* 46(2):77–92.

Forest, D. V. 1962. "High School Underachievers in College." *Journal of Educational Research,* 61(December):147–150.

Froomkin, J. and Pfeferman, M. No date. "A Computer Model to Measure the Requirements for Student Aid in Higher Education." Office of Program Planning and Evaluation, Office of Education, Department of Health, Education and Welfare.

Gable, R. I. 1957. "A Study of the Student Drop-Out Problem at Miami University," *Dissertation Abstracts,* 17:16.

Gadzella, B. M. 1967. "Factors Influencing Students to Withdraw from College." *College Student Survey,* 1(2):55–60.

Gadzella, B. M. 1968. "Characteristics of College Returnees." *College Student Survey,* 2(3):60–64.

Gadzella, B. M. and Bentall. 1967. "Differences in High School Academic Achievements and Mental Abilities of College Graduates and College Dropouts." *College and University,* 42(Spring):351–356.

Garner, W. C. 1970. "Crisis Intervention Technique with Potential College Dropouts." *Personnel and Guidance Journal,* 48(7):552–60.

Gehoski, N. and Schwartz, S. 1961. "Student Mortality and Related Factors." *Journal of Educational Research,* 54(January):192–194.

Gelso, J. and Rowell, D. 1967. "Academic Adjustment and the Persistence of Students with Marginal Academic Potential." *Journal of Counseling Psychology,* 14(5):478–481.

Gerritz, H. G. J. 1956. "The Relationship of Certain Personal and Socio-Economic Data to Success of Resident Freshmen Enrolled in the College of Science, Literature, and the Arts at the University of Minnesota." *Dissertation Abstracts,* 2366.

Goetz, W. and Leach, D. 1967. "Disappearing Student." *Personnel and Guidance Journal,* **45**(9):883–887.

Gold, B. K. 1970. "Academic Performance of Financial Aid Recipients, 1969–1970." *EDO45080.*

Goldsen, R. K. et al. 1960. *What College Students Think.* Princeton, N. J.: Van Nostrand Reinhold.

Gonyea, G. B. 1964. "Follow-Up of Above Average Students Who Leave the University of Texas." Research Report No. 16, The University of Texas Testing and Counseling Center, March.

Grace, H.A. 1957. "Personality Factors and College Attrition." *Peabody Journal of Education,* **35**:36–40.

Grande, P.P. and Simmons, J. B. 1967. "Personal Values and Academic Performance Among Engineering Students." *Personnel and Guidance Journal,* **46**:585–588.

Greenfield, L. B. 1964, "Attrition Among First Semester Engineering Freshmen." *The Personnel and Guidance Journal,* **52**(June):1003–1010.

Greive, D. E. 1970. "A Study of Student Attrition. Part I. Cuyahoga Community college, Cleveland, Ohio." *EDO38976.*

Gurin, G. et al. 1968. "Characteristics of Entering Freshmen Related to Attrition in the Literary College of a Large State University." Final Report, University of Michigan, Project No. 1938, U. S. Office of Education.

Gustavus, T. 1972. "Successful Students, Readmitted Student, and Dropouts." *Social Science Quarterly,* **53**(1):136–144.

Hackman, J. R. and Dysinger, W. S. 1970. "Reactions to College Withdrawal." *Journal of Experimental Education,* **39**(3):23–31.

Hackman, J. R. and Dysinger, W. S. 1970. "Research Notes: Commitment to College as a Factor in Student Attrition." *Sociology of Education,* **43**(3):311–324.

Halladay, D. W. and Andrew, D. C. 1958. "Dropouts from Arkansas College." *The Personnel and Guidance Journal,* **37**(November):212–213.

Hanks, C. J. 1954. "A Comparative Study of Factors Related to Retention and Withdrawal of Freshmen Students at the University of Arkansas." *Dissertation Abstracts,* **14**:1171.

Hannah, W. 1967. "Differences Between Drop-Outs and Stay-Ins at Entrance—1965 Freshmen." (Mimeograph), Project on Student Development, Plainfield, Vt., August.

Hannah, W. 1969a. *Dropout–Stayin Personality Differentials and College Environments.* (Dissertation). Ann Arbor: University Microfilms.

Hannah, W. 1969b. "The Leaver's View." *EDO29628.*

Hannah, W. 1969c. "Withdrawal from College." *Journal of College Personnel,* **10**(6):397–402.

Hannah, W. 1970a. "Collaborative Action with Outside Resource," *Institutional Research and Communication in Higher Education.* Tallahassee, Florida: Association for Institutional Research.

Hannah, W. 1970b. "Dropouts—Recent Studies: Implications and Observations." in O. Herron, (Ed.), *New Dimensions in Student Personnel Administration.* Scranton, Pa.: International Book Company.

References   121

Hannah, W. 1970c. "Dropout–Stayin Personality Differentials and College Environments." *Dissertation Abstracts International*, **31**(2–A):584.

Hannah, W. 1971. "Personality Differentials Between Lower Division Dropouts and Stay-Ins." *Journal of College Student Personnel*, **12**(1):16–19.

Hannah, W. and McCormick, J. 1970. *Report on College Attrition*. Plainfield, Vermont: Project on Student Development, Goddard College.

Hanson, G. and Taylor, R. 1970. "Interaction of Ability and Personality: Another Look at the Drop-Out Problem in an Institute of Technology." *Journal of Counseling Psychology*, **17**:540–545.

Hardie, V.S. and Anderson, J. R. 1971. "College Students; A Revealing Comprehensive Seven Year Study of 1106 College Freshmen. Attrition, Graduation, and Follow-up, Clemson University." *EDO55300.*

Harvey, J. 1970. "Preventing College Dropouts: A Review." *EDO43799.*

Hedley, W. 1968. "Freshmen Survival and Attrition at a Small, Private Liberal Arts College: A Discriminant Analysis of Intellectual and Non-Intellectual Variables." *Dissertation Abstracts*, **29**(2–A):461.

Heilbrun, A. B. 1964. "Personality Factors in College Dropouts." *Journal of Applied Psychology*, **49**(February):1–6.

Hempel, C. G. 1963. "Typological Methods in the Social Sciences." In Natanson, (Ed.), *Philosophy of the Social Sciences: A Reader*. New York: Random House.

Hendlin, H. 1972. "The Psychodynamics of Flunking Out." *Journal of Nervous and Mental Disease*, August: 131–143.

Hessel, W. Circa 1964. "A Study of the Relationship of the Omnibus Personality Inventory and College Performance." Unpublished manuscript, University of California, Berkeley, Center for the Study of Higher Education.

Hill, A. H. 1966. "Longitudinal Study of Attrition Among High Aptitude College Students." *Journal of Educational Research*, **60**(December):166–173.

Hirsch, S. J. and Keniston, K. 1970. "Psychological Issues in Talented College Dropouts." *Psychiatry*, **33**(1):1–20.

Hoffman, P. W. 1971. "A Comparative Study of Study Retention and Attrition at Manchester College." *Dissertation Abstracts International*, **32**(2–A):738.

Holmes, C. H. 1959. "Why They Left College." *College and University*, **34**(Spring):295–300.

Hood, A. B. 1957. "Certain Non-Intellectual Factors Related to Student Attrition at Cornell University." *Dissertation Abstracts*, 2919.

Horner, M. S. 1969. "Women's Will to Fail." *Psychology Today*, **3**(36):62.

Howard, J. 1969. "The Hippie College Dropout. Final Report." *EDO27853.*

Hoyt, D. P. 1959. "Size of High School and College Grades." *Personnel and Guidance Journal*, **37**:569–573.

Huber, W. H. 1971. "Channeling Students for Greater Retention." *College & University*, **47**(1):19–29.

Hughes, H. G. et al. No date. "A Follow-Up Study on Discontinuing Students at Grossmont College." *EDO19085.*

Iffert, R. E. 1954. "What Ought Colleges and Universities Do About Students Mortality?" *Current Issues in Higher Education*, 170–180.

·ert, R. E. 1956. "Study of College Student Retention and Withdrawal." *College and University*, **31**:435–437.

Iffert, R. E. 1957. "Retention and Withdrawal of College Students." U. S. Department of Health, Education and Welfare, Bulletin No. 1. Washington, D. C.: U. S. Government Printing Office.

Iffert, R. E. and Clarke, B. S. 1965. *College Applicants, Entrants, Dropouts,* Office of Education, U. S. Department of Health, Education and Welfare, FS5:54034.

Iowa State University. 1959. *A Study of Student Persistence at the State University of Iowa.* Iowa City: Office of the Registrar.

Irvine, D. W. 1965. "Graduation and Withdrawal; An Eight-Year Follow-Up." *College and University,* **40**(1):32–40.

Irvine, D. W. 1966. "Multiple Prediction of College Graduation From Pre-Admission Data." *The Journal of Experimental Education,* **35**(Fall):84–89.

Ivey, E. A. et al. 1966. "Personality Record as a Predictor of a College Attrition: A Discrimination Analysis." *College and University,* **41**(2):199–205.

Jaffe, A. J. and Adams, W. 1970. "Academic and Socio-Economic Factors Related to Entrance and Retention at Two and Four Year Colleges in the Late 1960's." *EDO49679.*

Jaffe, A. J. and Adams, W. 1971a. "1970–1971 Technical Progress Report, Follow-Up of Cross Section of 1965–1966 High School Seniors." Mimeograph. New York: Bureau of Applied Social Research.

Jaffe, A. J. and Adams, W. 1971b. "Open Admissions and Academic Quality." *Change,* **11**:78.

Jaffe, A. J. and Adams, W. 1972a. "1971–1972 Progress Report and Findings, Follow-Up of Cross-Section of 1965–1966 High School Seniors and Related Higher Educational Materials." (Mimeograph). New York: Bureau of Applied Social Research.

Jaffe, A. J. and Adams, W. 1972b. "Two Models of Open Enrollment." In Wilson and Mills, (eds.), *Universal Higher Education: Costs, Benefits, Options.* Washington, D. C.: American Council on Education.

Jencks, C. 1968. "Social Stratification and Higher Education." *Harvard Educational Review,* **38**:277–316.

Jencks, C. and Riesman, D. 1968. *The Academic Revolution,* New York. Doubleday.

Jencks, C. et al. 1972. *Inequality: A Reassessment of the Effect of Family and Schooling in America.* New York: Basic Books.

Jervis, F. M. and Congdon, R. C. 1958. "Student and Faculty Perceptions of Educational Values." *The American Psychologist,* **13**(August):464–466.

Johansson, C. B. and Rossman, J. E. 1973. "Persistence at a Liberal Arts College: A Replicated 5-Year Longitudinal Study." *Journal of Counseling Psychology,* **20**(1):1–9.

Johnson, D. E. 1970. "Personality Characteristics in Relation to College Persistence." *Journal of Counseling Psychology,* **17**(2):162–167.

Johnson, E. 1976. "A Comparison of Academically Successful and Unsuccessful College of Education Freshmen on Two Measures of Self." *Dissertation Abstracts,* **28**(4-A):1298.

Johnson, G. B., Jr. 1954. "Proposed Technique for Analysis of Drop-Outs at a State College." *Journal of Educational Research,* **47**(January).

Jones, E. S. 1955. "The Probation Student: What He Is Like and What Can Be Done About It." *Journal of Educational Research,* **49**:93–102.

Jones, G. and Dennison, J. D. 1972. "A Comparative Study of Persister and Non-Persister College Students." *EDO62975.*

References   123

Jones, J. B. 1962. "Some Personal-Social Factors Contributing to Academic Failure at Texas Southern University." *Personality Factors on College Campus.* Austin: Hogg Foundation for Mental Health.

Jones, R. 1970. "The Effects of Grouping Practices in a Community Junior College on Student Dropout, Achievement and Attitudes." *Dissertation Abstracts International,* 30(11-A):4722.

Kamens, D. H. 1967. "Social Class, College Contexts, and Education Attainment: Social Class and College Dropout." *EDO25795.*

Kamens, D. H. 1971. "The College 'Charter' and College Size: Effects on Occupational Choice and College Attrition." *Sociology of Education,* 44(3):270–296.

Kamens, D. H. 1972. "The Effects of College on Student Dropout. Final Report." *EDO68038.*

Karabel, J. 1972. "Community Colleges and Social Stratification." *Harvard Educational Review,* 42:521–562.

Karabel, J. and Astin, A. W. 1972. "Social Class, Academic Ability and College 'Quality.'" Unpublished paper, Office of Research, American Council on Education.

Keenan, C. and Holmes, J. 1970. "Predicting Graduation, Withdrawal, and Failure in College by Multiple Discriminant Analysis." *Journal of Educational Measurement,* 7:91–95.

Kendall, M. 1964. "Those Who Failed: Part 1." *Universities Quarterly,* 18:398–406; "Part 2." *Ibid.,* 19:69–77.

Keniston, K. 1968. *Young Radicals.* New York: Harcourt Brace Jovanovich.

Keniston, K. and Helmreich, R. 1965. "An Exploratory Study of Discontent and Potential Dropouts at Yale." (Mimeograph).

Kesselman, J. In press. *Stopping Out.* New York: M. Evans Company.

Kester, D. L. 1971b. "One Lesson from the Three-Year Norcal Attrition Study: Many of the Potential Dropouts Can Be Helped. Phase III, Final Report." *EDO57779.*

Kievit, M. B. 1971. "Expectations for Learning Environments and Personality Factors of Students Compared to Dropouts from 2-Year Institutions." *EDO47667.*

Kimney, R. G. 1971. "The Effect of Scholarship Aid Upon the Academic Achievement and Persistence of Washington State University Undergraduates." *Dissertation Abstracts International,* 31:(8-A):3903.

Knoell, D. 1960. "Institutional Research on Retention and Withdrawal." In H. T. Sprague, (Ed.), *Research on College Students.* Boulder, Colo.: The Western Interstate Commission for Higher Education; and Berkeley, Calif.: The Center for the Study of Higher Education, pp. 41–65.

Knoell, D. 1966. "A Critical Review of Research on the College Dropout." In L. A. Pervin et al., (eds.), *The College Dropout and the Utilization of Talent.* Princeton, N. J.: Princeton University Press.

Knop, E. 1967. "From a Symbolic-Interactionist Perspective: Some Notes on College Dropouts." *Journal of Educational Research,* 61(July):450–452.

Koelsche, C. L. 1956. "A Study of the Student Drop-Out Problem at Indiana University." *Journal of Educational Research,* 61(July):450–452.

Koelsche, C. L. 1956. "A Study of the Student Drop-Out Problem at Indiana University." *Journal of Educational Research,* 49:357–364.

Koester, N. 1968. "The Effects of Experimentally Induced Involvement upon Identified

Potential College Dropouts with Respect to Dropout Rate, Academic Achievement, and Participation in Extra-Curricular Activities." *Dissertation Abstracts,* **29**(6-A):1756.

Kooker, E. and Bellamy, R. 1969. "Some Background Differences Between College Graduates and Dropouts." *Psychology,* **6**(4):1–6.

Kooker, E. and Bellamy, R. 1969. "Some Psychometric Differences Between Graduates and Dropouts." *Psychology,* **6**(2):65–70.

Kramer, L. and Kramer, M. "The College Library and the Dropout." *College and Research Libraries,* **29**(4):310.

Krebs, R. E. and Liberty, P. G., Jr. 1971. "A Comparative Study of Three Groups of Withdrawal Students on Ten Factor Variables Derived From a 36 Problem Self-Report Inventory." *ED052690.*

Kubie, L. S. 1965. "Various Aspects of the Dropout Problem." *Journal of Nervous and Mental Disease,* **141**(4):395–402.

Kunhart, W. E. and Roleder, G. 1964. "Counseling Techniques With Potential Dropout Students in Junior College." *Journal of Counseling Psychology,* **11**(2).

Kuznik, A. 1973. "Reverse Transfers from University to Community College." *Journal of College Student Personnel,* **14**(May):250–253.

Landrith, H. F. 1971. "Prescription for Junior College Dropouts." *School and Society,* **99**(January):49–51.

Lansing, J. B., Lorimer, T., and Moriguchi, C. 1960. *How People Pay For College.* Ann Arbor: Survey Research Center.

Lavin, D. E. 1965. *The Prediction of Academic Performance.* New York: Russell Sage Foundation.

Lavin, D. E. 1974. "Student Retention and Graduation at the City University of New York: September 1970 Enrollees Through Seven Semesters." Mimeograph. Office of Research, August 1974 Report.

Lawhorn, J. T. 1971. "A Study of Persisters and Dropouts in the Secretarial Science Program at Miami-Dade Junior College." Doctoral dissertation, University of Miami.

Lembesis, A. C. 1965. "A Study of Students Who Withdrew from College During Their Second, Third or Fourth Years." Doctoral dissertation, University of Oregon.

Lenning, O. T. 1974. *The "Benefit Crisis" in Higher Education.* Washington, D. C.: American Association for Higher Education.

Levenson, E. and Kohn, M. 1964. "A Demonstration Clinic for College Dropouts." *College Health,* **12**:4, 382–391.

Lichter, S. O. et al. 1969. "Dropouts." Review in *Child Welfare,* October.

Lindsay, N. S. 1974. "Where Did You Go? Out! Office of Instructional Research and Evaluation." Mimeograph, Harvard University.

Lins, L. J. and Abell, A. P. 1965. "Attendance Patterns of Fall 1958 New Freshmen for Twelve Semesters After Entrance for the University of Wisconsin, Madison Campus." Madison: University of Wisconsin, pp. 1–31.

Lins, L. J. and Abell, A. P. 1966. "Followup of Fall 1958 Madison Campus New Freshmen Who Had Left the Madison Campus and Who Had Not Received a Degree from the Madison Campus Within Twelve Semesters After Entrance." Madison: University of Wisconsin, pp. 1–25.

Lins, L. J., Abell, A. P., and Hutchins, H. C. 1966. "Relative Usefulness in Predicting Academic Success of the ACT, the SAT, and Some Other Variables." *Journal of Experimental Education,* **35**(Winter):1–29.

Lins, L. J. and Pitt, H. 1953. "The Staying Power and Rate of Progress of University of Wisconsin Freshmen." *College and University,* **29**:86–99.

Little, J. K. 1959. "The Persistence of Academically Talented Youth in University Studies." *Educational Record,* (June):237–241.

Locke, C. 1970. "Small Group Counseling Compared with Freshman Orientation Classes in Reducing Attrition of Freshman Junior College Students." *Dissertation Abstracts International,* **31**(4-A):1576.

Lucas, J. A. 1974. "Follow-Up Study of 1969 and 1971 Alumni." Office of Planning and Research, William Rainey Harper College, March 1.

McClelland, D. C. et al. 1968. *Talent and Society.* Princeton: Van Nostrand Reinhold.

Mack, F. 1973. "Predicting College Persistence for Educational Opportunity Students." *Psychology,* **10**(February):14–28.

McKeachie, W. J. and Lin, Y. G. 1971. "Sex Differences in Student Response to College Teachers." *American Educational Research Journal,* **8**(2):221–226.

MacLachlan, P. S. and Burnett, C. W. 1954. "Who Are the Superior Freshmen in College?" *The Personnel and Guidance Journal,* **34**:345–349.

McMammon, W. H., Jr. 1965. "The Use of Non-Intellectual Variables in Predicting Attrition of Academically Capable Students at the University of Tennessee." Doctoral dissertation, University of Tennessee.

MacMillan, T. F. 1969a. "Establishing a Predictive Model for Early Recognition of Potential Community College Student Attrition." *EDO44102.*

MacMillan, T. F. 1969b. "NorCal Project: Phase I, Final Report." *EDO31240.*

MacMillan, T. F. 1970a. "NorCal Project: Phase II, Final Report." *EDO39879.*

MacMillan, T. F. 1970b. "NorCal: The Key Is Cooperation." *Junior College Journal,* **40**:28–31.

McNeely, J. J. 1938. *College Student Mortality.* Washington, D. C.: U. S. Office of Education, Bulletin 1937, No. 11.

Maier, R. O. 1971. "Some Variations in Probabilities of Success, Failure and Dropout." *EDO50720.*

Malloy, J. 1954. "An Investigation of Scholastic Over- and Under-Achievement Among Female College Freshmen." *Journal of Counseling Psychology,* **1**:260–263.

Margolis, J. 1969. "Non-Dropout Problem." *Journal of Higher Education,* **40**(5):394–397.

Marks, E. 1967. "Student Perceptions of College Persistence, and Their Intellective, Personality and Performance Correlates." *Journal of Educational Psychology,* **58**(4):210–221.

Marsh, L. M. 1966. "College Dropouts: A Review." *Personnel and Guidance Journal,* **44**(5):475–481.

Marsh, L. M. 1969. "The Development of an Education Values Scale for the Prediction of College Dropouts Using Ritter's Social Learning Theory as a Theoretical Construct." *Dissertation Abstracts International,* **30**(3-A):988.

Max, P. 1968. "How Many Graduate CUNY." *EDO26954.*

Medsker, L. L. and Trent, J. W. 1965. *The Influence of Different Types of Public Higher Institutions on College Attendance from Varying Socioeconomic and Ability Levels.* Center for the Study of Higher Education, University of California, Berkeley.

Medsker, L. L. and Trent, J. W. 1968. *Beyond High School.* San Francisco: Jossey-Bass.

Mehra, N. 1973. *Retention and Withdrawal of University Students.* Office of Institutional Research, University of Alberta, December.

Mercer, M. 1941. "Study of Student Mortality in a Home Economics College." *Journal of Educational Research,* 34(March):531–537.

Merigold, R. A. 1967. "The Development and Testing of a Scale to Identify Male Dropouts at Liberal Arts Colleges." *EDO12388.*

Merigold, F. 1969. "A Scale to Identify Male Dropouts at Liberal Arts Colleges." *College Student Survey,* 3(1):19–22.

Merrill, K. E. 1964. "The Relationship of Certain Non-Intellectual Factors to Lack of Persistence of Higher Ability Students at the University of California, Berkeley." Doctoral dissertation, University of California, Berkeley.

Meskill, V. 1971. "Success or Academic Failure." *Journal of the National Association of College Admission Counselors,* 15(4):15.

Meyer, J. 1970. "High School Effects on College Intentions." *American Journal of Sociology,* 76:59–70.

"Michigan Center Gives Dropouts a Second Chance." 1971. *College Management,* 56 (April).

Miller, G. W. 1973–1974. "Student Drop-Out and Wastage: A Comparison Between Australian and British Universities." *The Australian University,* Part I, 11(November 1973):239–250; Par II, 12(May 1974):3–25.

Milton, O., Ed. 1966. "Proceedings: A Conference on Student Retention in Tennessee College and University." *EDO44084.*

Mitchell, J. A. 1968. "A Study of Full Time Students Who Discontinued Their Attendance at A. W. C. After Attending One or Both Semesters of the 1966–67 School Year." *EDO24360.*

Mock, K. R. and Young G. 1969. "Students' Intellectual Attitudes, Aptitude, and Persistence at the University of California." *EDO32862.*

Morgan, M. 1971. "The OPI, the ACT and University Attrition: A Discriminant Analysis." *Dissertation Abstracts International,* 31(8-A):3906.

Morgenstern, M. and Stronzin, H. 1970. "A Study of Student Dropouts from Vocationally Oriented Business Programs at Nassau Community College." *EDO44100.*

Morishima, J. K. 1968. Analysis of Probations and Drops for Students Entering in 1962–1963, University of Washington, Office of Institutional Educational Research, Report No. 143–4.

Morrisey, R. J. 1971. "Attrition in Probationary Freshmen." *Journal of College Student Personnel,* 12(4):279–285.

Morrison, J. L. and Ferrante, R. 1973. "Why the Disadvantaged Drop Out: The Administrators' View." *EDO71665.*

Mukherjee, C. 1958. "Characteristics of Honor Graduates at the University of Nebraska." *Dissertation Abstracts,* 499–500.

Mullally, Robert R. 1967. "A Study to Determine the Dropout Rate and the Reasons Why Academically-Able Students Withdrew from the University of Wyoming During the Period, the Beginning of Fall Semester 1963 to the Beginning of Fall Semester 1964." *EDO30814.*

Munday, L. A. and Davis J. 1974. *Assessment of Adult Accomplishment.* Iowa City: American College Testing.

Munger, P. F. 1957. "Can We Really Predict Who Will Graduate From College?" *College and University*, **32**(Winter):218–221.

Musgrave, M. 1971. "Failing Minority Students: Class, Caste and Racial Bias in American Colleges." *College Composition and Communication*, **22**(1):24–29.

Nasatir, D. 1969. "A Contextual Analysis of Academic Failure. *School Review*, **71**(3):290–298.

Nelson, A. G. 1966. "College Characteristics Associated with Freshman Attrition." *Personnel and Guidance Journal*, **44**(10):1046–1050.

Nelson, J. 1972. "High School Context and College Plans: The Impact of Social Structure on Aspirations." *American Sociological Review*, **37**:143–148.

Newcomb, T. M. and Flacks, R. 1964. *Deviant Subcultures on a College Campus*. Ann Arbor: University of Michigan.

Newman, F. et al. 1971. *Report on Higher Education*. U.S. Department of Health, Education and Welfare: Office of Education.

Nicholi, A. 1970. "An Investigation of Harvard Dropouts, Final Report." *EDO42068*.

Nicholson, E. 1973. "Predictors of Graduation from College." *ACT Research Report*, 56.

O'Donnell, P. 1968. "Predictors of Freshman Academic Success and Their Relationship to Attrition." *Dissertation Abstracts*, **39**(3-A):798.

Oklahoma State Regents for Higher Education. 1964. *In and Out of College*. Oklahoma City: State Regents for Higher Education.

Omnibus Personality Inventory: Research Manual. 1962. University of California, Berkeley, Center for the Study of Higher Education.

O'Shea, A. J. 1969. "Peer Relationships and Male Academic Achievement: A Review and Suggested Clarification." *Personnel and Guidance Journal*, **47**:417–423.

Otto, D. 1966. "A Study of Students Who Withdrew from the University of Michigan's College of Literature, Science, and the Arts." (Draft), October 3.

Otto, D. and Cope R. G. 1965. "A Study of Students Who Voluntarily Withdrew from the University of Michigan's College of Literature, Science, and the Arts." Ann Arbor: Office of Institutional Research.

Pace, C. R. 1963. *College and University Environmental Scales: Preliminary Technical Manual*. Princeton: Educational Testing Service.

Pace, C. R. and Stern, G. G. 1958. "An Approach to the Measurement of Psychological Characteristics of College Environments." *Journal of Educational Psychology*, **49**:269–277.

Pandey, R. E. 1972. "Personality Characteristics of Successful, Dropout and Probationary Black and White University Students." *Journal of Counseling Psychology*, **19**(5):382–386.

Panos, R. J. and Astin, A. W. 1967. "Attrition Among College Students." *ACE Research Reports*, **2**(4). Also *EDO14113*.

Panos, R. J. and Astin A. W. 1968. "Attrition Among College Students." *American Educational Research Journal*, **5**:57–72.

Pattishall, E. G., Jr. and Banghart, F. W., Jr. 1957. "A Comparative Analysis of School of Education Graduates and Withdrawals." *Educational Research Bulletin*. University of Virginia, April.

Patton, B. K., Jr. 1958. "A Study of Drop-Outs from the Junior Division of Louisiana State University, 1953–55." *Dissertation Abstracts*, 484–485.

Pearlman, S. 1962. "An Investigation of the Problem of Academic Underachievement

Among Intellectually Superior College Students." In Sanford, (Ed.), *The American College.* New York: Wiley.

Pervin, L. A. 1965. "Counseling the College Dropout." *Journal of College Placement,* **26**(October):30–31.

Pervin, L. A. 1965. "A New Look at College Drop-outs." *University: A Princeton Quarterly,* Winter.

Pervin, L. A. 1966. "The Later Academic, Vocational, and Personal Success of College Dropouts." In L. Pervin et al., (Eds.), *The College Dropout and the Utilization of Talent.* Princeton: Princeton University Press.

Pervin, L. A. 1967. "Dissatisfaction with College and the College Dropout: A Transactional Approach." *EDO21335.*

Pervin, L. A. and Rubin, D. B. 1967. "Student Dissatisfaction with College and the College Dropout: A Transactional Approach." *Journal of Social Psychology,* **72**:285–295.

Pervin, L. A. et al., (Eds.) 1966. *The College Dropout and the Utilization of Talent.* Princeton: Princeton University Press.

Peterson, D. 1967. "A Longitudinal Study of Nonintellective Characteristics of College Dropouts." *Dissertation Abstracts,* **28**(6-A):2076.

Peterson, R. E. 1965. "On a Typology of College Students." *Research Bulletin.* Princeton: Educational Testing Service, pp. 65–69.

Petrik, N. D. 1967. "Socio-Economic Status, Vocational Interests, and Persistence in Selected College Curricula." *Vocational Guidance Quarterly,* **16**(1):39–44.

Phi Delta Kappan, March, 1965:311.

Phillips, D. L. 1966. "Deferred Gratification in a College Setting: Some Costs and Gains." *Social Problems,* **13**:333–343.

Pitcher, R. W. 1969. "Helping to Salvage the College Failout." *EDO29575.*

Pitcher, R. W. and Blaushild, B. 1972. *Why College Students Fail.* Review in *Journal of Higher Education,* **42**(4):1972.

Pope, L. 1970. *The Right College.* New York: Macmillan.

Prediger, D. J. 1965. "Prediction of Persistence in College." *Journal of Counseling Psychology,* **12**(Winter):62–67.

Pulcrano, O. 1969. "The Class of 1960: A Study of the College Survival Rate." *School Counselor,* **16**(4):277–281.

Reboussin, R. 1969. "Trends and Issues at Belvit College, Report No. 3: The Class of 1972." *EDO33651.*

Reed, H. B. 1968. "College Students' Motivation Related to Voluntary Dropout and Under-Achievement; College Assessment Inventory." *Journal of Educational Research,* **62**(May):412–416.

Reik, L. E. 1966. "The College Dropout in Clinical Perspective." In L. Pervin et al., (Eds.), *The College Dropout and the Utilization of Talent.* Princeton: Princeton University Press, pp. 177–187.

Rice, G. A. 1969. "An Examination of the Earned Grade Distribution Between 'Successful' and 'Dropout' Students at Yakima Valley College." *EDO36293.*

Richling, J. 1971. "70 Per Cent." *University Quarterly,* **25**(Spring):135–138.

Roa, C. O. 1966. "An Investigation of Factors Leading to the Withdrawal of Waldorf Junior College Freshmen." *Dissertation Abstracts,* **27**(3A):681.

References   **129**

Robin, B. and Johnson, P. 1969. "Identifying Potential Dropouts with Class Lists: College Students." *Improving College and University Teaching*, **17**(3):178–179.

Robinson, L. F. 1967. "Relation of Student Persistence in College to Satisfaction with 'Environmental' Factors." Doctoral dissertation, University of Arkansas.

Robinson, L. F. 1969. "Relation of Student Persistence in College to Satisfaction with Environmental Factor." *Journal of Educational Research*, **62**(1):6–10.

Rock, D. et al. 1970. "Relationships Between College Characteristics and Student Achievement." *American Educational Research Association*, **7**:109–121.

Rootman, I. 1972. "Voluntary Withdrawal from a Total Adult Socialization Organization: A Model." *Sociology of Education*, **45**:258–270.

Rose, H. A. 1965. "Prediction and Prevention of Freshman Attrition." *Journal of Counseling Psychology*, **13**(Summer):399–403.

Rose, H. A. and Elton, C. F. 1966. "Another Look at the College Dropout." *Journal of Counseling Psychology*, **13**(Summer): 242–245.

Rossman, J. E. et al. 1975. *Open Admissions at City University of New York: An Analysis of the First Year*. New York: Prentice-Hall.

Rossman, J. E. and Kirk, B. A. 1970. "Factors Related to Persistence and Withdrawal Among University Students." *Journal of Counseling Psychology*, **17**(January):56–62.

Rutkevich, M. N. 1966. "Why a Student Does Not Arrive at the Finish." *Soviet Education*, **8**(January):28–37.

Ryle, A. 1969. *Student Casualties*. London: Penguin.

Ryle, A. 1971. "Student Health and Student Wastage." *University Quarterly*, **25**(Spring):162–168.

Samenow, S. E. 1967. "Studying the College Dropout." *Teachers College Record*, **68**(May):640 49.

Sarnoff, I. and Raphael, T. 1955. "Five Failing College Students." *American Journal of Orthopsychiatry*, **25**:343–372.

Savicki, V., Schumer, H., and Stanfield, R. 1970. "Student Role Orientations and College Dropouts." *Journal of Counseling Psychology*, **17**:559–566.

Schoemer, J. 1968. "The College Pushout." *Personnel and Guidance Journal*, **46**(7):677.

Schöen, W. T., Jr. 1974. "Student Reactions to College: Users Manual." Princeton: Educational Testing Service, August.

Scott, J. C. 1971. "A Study of the Relationship Between Students' Personal Perception of Environmental Press and Attrition at a Two-Year College." Doctoral dissertation, University of Missouri, Columbia.

Selby, J. E. 1973. "Relationships Existing Among Race, Student Financial Aid, and Persistence in College." *Journal of College Student Personnel*, **14**(1):38–40.

Sensor, P. 1967. "Follow-Up of 1965 Freshmen Who Did Not Return For Fall Semester 1966." *EDO14987*.

Sewell, W. and Shah, V. 1967. "Socioeconomic Status, Intelligence, and the Attainment of Higher Education." *Sociology of Education*, **40**:1–23.

Sewell, W. and Wegner, E. 1970. "Selection and Context as Factors Affecting the Probability of Graduation from College." *American Journal of Sociology*, **75**:665, 679.

Sexton, V. S. 1965. "Factors Contributing to Attrition in College Populations: Twenty-five Years of Research." *Journal of General Psychology*, **72**(2):301–326.

Shaw, M. C. and Brown, D. J. 1957. "Scholastic Underachievement of Bright College Student." *Personnel and Guidance Journal*, **36**:195–199.

Sheeder, F. I. 1939. "Student Losses in a Liberal Arts College." *Journal of American Association of College Registrars*, **15**:34–40.

Shrier, I. and Lavin, D. E. 1974. *Open Admissions: A Bibliography for Research and Application*. City University of New York, Office of Program and Policy Research.

Sidles, C. 1969. "The Relationship of Changes in Freshman Perceptions of Campus Environments to College Achievements and Attrition." *Dissertation Abstracts*, **29**(11-A):3844.

Skaling, M. M. 1971. "Review of the Research Literature." In R. Cope et al., Eds., *An Investigation of Entrance Characteristics Related to Types of College Dropouts*. United States Office of Education, Final Research Report, pp. 17–60.

Skaling, M. M. 1969. "An Exploratory Study of Twenty Types of College Dropouts and Stay-Ins Using Social and Psychological Variables." Masters thesis prospectus, Graduate School, University of Massachusetts, Amherst, Mass. May.

Slater, J. M. 1960. "Influence on Students' Perception and Persistence in Undergraduate College." *Journal of Educational Research*, **54**(September):3–8.

Slocum, W. L. 1956. *Academic Mortality at the State College of Washington*. Pullman: State College of Washington.

Smith, J. S. 1971. "A Multivariate Combination of Academic and Non-Academic Factors Related to Student Attrition." Doctoral dissertation, University of Pittsburgh.

Smithers, A. G. 1972. "Factors in the Success and Failure of Students." In *Proceedings*. London: Society for Research into Higher Education, pp. 16–34.

Smithers, A. G. and Batcock, A. 1970. "Success and Failures Among Social Scientists and Health Scientists at a Technological University." *The British Journal of Educational Psychology*, **40**(June):144–153.

Smithers, A. G. and Dann, S. 1974. "Success and Failure Among Engineers, Physical Scientists and Linguists at a Technological University." *British Journal of Educational Psychology*, **44**(November):189–193.

Snyder, F. A. and Blocker, E. 1970. "A Profile of Non-Persisting Students: A Description of Educational Goals and Achievements, Activities, and Perceptions of Non-Graduates, Spring 1969. Research Report No. 3." *EDO37218.*

Spady, W. G. 1967. "Educational Mobility and Access: Growth and Paradoxes." *American Journal of Sociology*, **73**:273–286.

Spady, W. G. 1970. "Dropouts from Higher Education: An Interdisciplinary Review and Synthesis," *Interchange*, **1**(April):64–85.

Spady, W. G. 1971. "Dropouts from Higher Education: Toward an Empirical Model." *Interchange*, **2**:38–62.

Starr, A. et al. 1972. "Differences in College Student Satisfaction: Academic Dropouts, Non-Academic Dropouts, and Non Dropouts." *Journal of Counseling Psychology*, **19**(4):318–322.

Stern, G. G. 1970. *People in Context*. New York: Wiley.

Stern, G. G. et al. 1956. *Methods in Personality Assessment*. Glencoe, Ill.: Free Press.

Stier, W. F., Jr. 1971. "Student-Athlete Attrition Among Selected Liberal Arts Colleges." *EDO58834.*

Stone, D. B. 1965. "Predicting Student Retention and Withdrawal in a Selected State University College of New York." Doctoral dissertation, Cornell University.

Stordahl, K. E. 1967. "Student Perceptions of Their Voluntary Withdrawal from Northern." Office of Institutional Research, Northern Michigan University, October.

References

Stordahl, K. E. 1970. "Influence on Voluntary Withdrawal from College." *College and University*, 45(2):163–171.

Suczek, R. F. and Alfert, E. 1966. "Personality Characteristics of College Dropouts." *EDO10101*.

Suddarth, B. M. 1957. "Factors Influencing the Graduation of Freshmen Who Enroll at Purdue University." Unpublished report, June.

Summerskill, J. 1962. "Dropouts from College." In N. Sanford, (Ed.), *The American College*. New York: Wiley, pp. 627–657.

Summerskill, J. and Darling, C. E. 1955. "Sex Differences in Adjustment to College." *Journal of Counseling Psychology*, 46:355–361.

Taylor, R. G. and Hanson, G. 1970. "Interest and Persistence." *Journal of Counseling Psychology*, 17:506–509.

Taylor, R. G. et al. 1967. "Interest Patterns of Successful and Non-successful Male Collegiate Technical Students." *Journal of Educational Research*, 60(May):401–402.

Taylor, R. G. et al. 1971. "Experimental Housing and Tutoring: Effects on Achievement and Attrition." *Journal of College Student Personnel*. 12(4):271–278.

Tennessee College Association. 1972. *Student Retention—Attrition, Entering Freshmen—Fall 1968, Report No. 4*. Tennessee College Association, Center for Higher Education.

Thayer, R. E. 1971. "Do Low Grades Cause College Students to Give Up?" *EDO54725*.

Theus, R. 1971. "The Miseducated Dropout." *College Student Journal*. 5(November–December):119–120.

Thistlethwaite, D. L. 1959. "College Press and Student Achievement." *Journal of Educational Psychology*, 50:183–191.

Thistlethwaite, D. L. 1963. *Recruitment and Retention of Talented College Students*. Cooperative Research Project with the United States Office of Education, January.

Thompson, M. 1953. "Admission Information as Predictors for Graduation." Unpublished master's thesis, Cornell University.

Timmons, F. 1972. "Personality and Demographic Factors Associated with Freshman Withdrawal from College." *Dissertation Abstracts International*, 33(4-B):1808–1809.

Tinto, V. 1971. "The Effect of College Accessibility Upon the Rates and Selectivity of College Attendance." Doctoral dissertation, University of Chicago.

Tinto, V. and Cullen, J. 1973. *Dropout in Higher Education: A Review and Theoretical Synthesis of Recent Research*. Mimeograph, Teachers College, Columbia.

Trent, J. W. et al. 1965. "Technology Education and Human Development." *Educational Record*, 46:93–103.

Trent, J. W. and Medsker, L. L. 1968. *Beyond High School*. San Francisco: Jossey-Bass.

Trent, J. and Ruyle, J. 1965. "Variation, Flow, and Patterns of College Attendance." *College and University*, 41:61–76.

Turner, H. J., Jr. 1970. "The Half that Leaves: A Limited Survey of Attrition in Community Colleges." *EDO38127*.

University of Chicago. 1965. "Grass Roots Talent Search Project." *Phi Delta Kappan*, March:311.

Van Alstine, C. 1973. "Attrition Rates of College Students." An unpublished paper. Washington, D. C.: American Council on Education.

Vaughan, R. P. 1968. "College Dropouts: Dismissed Vs. Withdrew." *Personnel and Guidance Journal*, 46(7):685–689.

Vreeland, R. and Bidwell, C. 1966. "Classifying University Departments: An Approach to the Analysis of Their Effects Upon Undergraduates' Values and Attitudes." *Sociology of Education*, 39:237–254.

Wagner, V. 1968. "Success, Failure, Level of Aspiration, and Self-Esteem." *ED025217*.

Wallace, W. L. 1966. Student Culture: *Social Structure and Continuity in a Liberal Arts College*. Chicago: Aldine.

Wallach, M. A. 1972. "The Psychology of Talent and Graduate Education." Paper presented at a conference on Cognitive Styles and Creativity, sponsored by the Graduate Record Examination Board, Montreal.

Waller, C. A. 1964. "Research Related to College Persistence." *College and University*, 38:281–294.

Warriner, C. C. et al. 1966. "Failure to Complete as Family Characteristics: A College Sample." *Journal of Educational Research*, 59(10)466–468.

Watley, D. J. 1964. "Type, Location, and Size of High School and Prediction of Achievement in an Institute of Technology." *Educational and Psychological Measurement*, 24:331–338.

Watley, D. J. 1965. "The Minnesota Counseling Inventory and Persistence in an Institute of Technology." *Journal of Counseling Psychology*, 12:94–97.

Wedge, B. 1958. *Psyco-Social Characteristics of College Men*. New Haven: Yale University Press.

Wegner, E. L. 1967. "The Relationship of College Characteristics to Graduation." Doctoral dissertation, University of Wisconsin.

Wegner, E. L. and Sewell, W. H. 1970. "Selection and Context As Factors Affecting the Probability of Graduation from College." *American Journal of Sociology*, 75(4):665–679.

Weigel, M. 1969. "A Comparison of Persisters and Non-Persisters in a Junior College." *ED044115*.

Weigrand, G. 1953. "Goal Aspirations and Academic Success." *Personnel and Guidance Journal*, 31:458–461.

Weigrand, G. 1957. "Adaptiveness and the Role of Parents in Academic Success." *Personnel and Guidance Journal*, 35:518–522.

Weintraub, R. G. and Salley, R. E. 1945. "Graduation Prospects of an Entering Freshman." *Journal of Educational Research*, 39(October):116–126.

Wenrich, W. et al. 1971. "Keeping Dropouts In: Retention of Students Identified as High Probability Dropouts." *ED047684*.

West, R. M. 1928. "Student Mortality, Student Survival, and Student Accounting." In E. Hudelson, (Ed.), *Problems of College Education*. Minneapolis: University of Minnesota Press.

Wharton, W. L. 1966. "Factors Associated With Success of Returning College Dropouts." *Dissertation Abstracts*, 27(3A):616.

White, J. H. 1971. "Individual and Environmental Factors Associated with Freshman Attrition at a Multi-Campus Community College." Doctoral dissertation, George Washington University.

Whittaker, D. 1971. "Psychological Adjustment of Intellectual, Non-Conformist Collegiate Dropouts." *Adolescence*, 6(Winter):415–424.

"Why Do College Freshmen Drop Out?" 1967. *American Education*, 4(June).

Wideman, J. W. 1966. "College Undergraduate Dropouts; Causes, Cures, and Implication for Secondary Schools." *National Association of Secondary Schools Principals' Bulletin,* **50**(April):224–234.

Williams, T. 1969. "Comparison of College Dropouts, Returnees, and Graduates on Selected High School Variables." *Dissertation Abstracts,* **29**(9A):2972.

Williams, V. 1966. "Difficulties in Identifying Relatively Permanent Characteristics Related to Persistence in College." *Journal of Counseling Psychology,* **13**(Spring).

Williams, V. 1967. "College Dropout; Qualities of His Environment." *Personnel and Guidance Journal,* **45**(9):878–882.

Willingham, W. W. and Findikyan, N. 1969. "Transfer Students: Who's Moving from Where to Where, and What Determines Who's Admitted." *College Board Review,* (Summer)4–11.

Wing, C. W. and Wallach, M. A. 1971. *College Admissions and the Psychology of Talent.* New York: Holt, Rinehart & Winston.

Winther, S. R. et al. 1969. "The Invisible Student: A Longitudinal Study of the Beginning Freshman Class of 1963 at the University of New Mexico." *EDO30532.*

Wishiewsky, W. 1969. "Some Factors Affecting Success at University." *Polish Sociological Bulletin,* **19**:59–73.

Withey, S. B. 1971. *A Degree and What Else.* New York: McGraw-Hill.

Wolford, M. E. 1964. "A Comparison of Dropouts and Persisters in a Private Liberal Arts College." Doctoral dissertation, University of Oregon.

Wood, P. J. 1963. "Correlates of Attrition and Academic Success." In Kenneth M. Wilson, (Ed.), *Research Related to College Admissions.* Atlanta: Southern Regional Education Board, pp. 89–105.

Wright, E. O. 1973. "A Study of Student Leaves of Absence." *Journal of Higher Education,* **44**(March):235–247.

Yartz, Larry J. 1974. "Student Attrition at Allegheny College." Report of the Office of Institutional Research, Allegheny College, Meadville, Pa.

Yonge, G. E. 1965. "Students; Persistence." *Review of Educational Research,* **35**(4):256–257.

Young, R. D. 1966. "Wipe Out Freshman Failures." *School and Community,* (December):10–11.

Yourglich, A. 1966. "A Four Phase Study of Value Homophily, Friendship, Social Participation, and College Dropouts." *Sociological Analysis,* **26**(1):19–26.

Yuker, H. E. et al. 1972. "Who Leaves Hofstra, For What Reasons." Research Report No. 102. Center for the Study of Higher Education, Hofstra University, May.

Zaccaria, L. and Creaser, J. 1971. "Factors Related to Persistence in an Urban Commuter University." *Journal of College Student Personnel,* **12**(July):286–291.

APPENDIX A THE PARADOX OF ACCESS

In higher education, growth has been used traditionally as a measure of progress. The number of students enrolled, the number of institutions in existence, and the amount of money being spent on higher education all indicate remarkable growth.

Between 1955 and 1965, the number of high school graduates increased more than 85 percent; the number of those graduates going on to college increased 110 percent.[1] Today more than half of our young people enter college; yet 20 years ago less than 25 percent entered.[2]

In the last two decades the total number of institutions of higher education has increased from 1,850 to nearly 2,500,[3] and average enrollment has doubled.[4]

Total higher education outlays, public and private, have been increasing at two-and-one-half times the rate of increase in the Gross National Product—which has itself grown nearly fourfold since 1950.[5]

The common plea of educators is that this growth be nurtured until we reach the goal of access to a college education for every young American, a goal finally within reach in several States.[6]

Yet access alone does not automatically lead to a successful education. It measures only the exposure of a particular age group to whatever educational institutions there are, and not the equality of the experience they are likely to find there. When the Task Force looked behind the growth statistics, they were found to mask a major phenomenon: the surprisingly large and growing number of students who voluntarily drop out of college.

Table 1 summarizes estimates of graduation rates by type of institution.[7]

These figures indicate that of the more than one million young people who enter college each year, fewer than half will complete 2 years of study, and only about one-third will ever complete a 4-year course of study. For example: at the University of Texas no more than 30 percent of entering students graduate in 4 years; after a 5th year the total is still less than 50 percent.[8] The California State College system recently reported that, as an average for all campuses, only 13 percent of entering freshmen graduate in

1

SOURCE. Frank Newman et al., *Report on Higher Education*, U.S. Department of Health, Education, and Welfare, Office of Education, March 1971.

4 years from the college they enter; the highest was 17 percent, the lowest
only 8 percent.[9]

TABLE 1.—*Variation in graduation rates according to selectivity of institutions*

Type of institution	Percentage of students graduating within 4 years at initial institution	Percentage graduating within 10 years at some institution	1st-time full-time enrollments, fall 1969	Percentage of all 1st-time, full-time enrollees
Fifteen most selective private universities........	80–85	90–95	20,000	1
Large State universities........	35–45	60–70	239,000	15
State colleges........	15–25	35–50	322,000	21
Public junior colleges...........	[1] 20–25	[2] 15–30	457,000	29

[1] Graduation from the 2-year program in a 2-year period.
[2] Graduation with a 4-year degree after transfer.

NOTE.—Remaining categories of institutions are: less selective private universities
(73,000 first-time enrollees, or 5%); 4-year private colleges (266,000 first-time enrollees,
or 17%); 2-year private colleges (55,000 first-time enrollees, or 4%); and small State
universities (116,000 enrollees, or 7%), or a total of 1.55 million first-time, full-time
enrollees.

The Significance of "Dropping Out"

"Dropping out" is a pejorative term, and, we think, unfortunately so.
Individuals should be able to "drop in" and "drop out" of college without
social stigma. Indeed, we feel that many students are too reluctant to leave
college, and that "hanging on" and "drifting" are themselves major problems in higher education.

Yet the fact that enormous numbers of students do drop out is an index
of utmost significance, and, we believe, an index which has escaped public
notice and educational debate. Laymen are generally astonished to hear
that most students who attend college never finish. Educators themselves
are often surprised when confronted with the numbers involved. But more
importantly, both laymen and educators assume that to the extent "dropping
out" is a problem, it is an individual, not an educational, problem. Girls
wish to marry, boys want to get jobs, and "many students are not suited
for college," anyway.

This view is at best only half-true. Many students do leave college for
personal reasons, such as shortage of money or the desire to get a job.

2

But the majority of dropouts cite dissatisfaction with college and the desire to reconsider personal goals and interests as the major reasons for leaving school.[10] After reviewing the studies on dropping out and interviewing scores of students, we are convinced that "dropouts" reveal an educational problem of considerable proportions. College is failing to capture the attention and engage the enthusiasm of many students. For some, it is a decidedly negative experience.

What makes this problem so acute is that the great expansion in higher education in recent years has been in just those institutions where dropout rates are the highest—in so-called unselective institutions. Selective institutions have rigorous admission procedures that, in effect, screen *in* only those who are likely to succeed. At such institutions, "dropping out" occurs in advance of admissions.

In interpreting these findings, we can assume that society fulfills its obligation simply by providing the opportunity for as many as possible to enter college. Success cannot and should not be guaranteed. High dropout rates are not inconsistent with our commitment to broad access, but rather reflect the maintenance of rigorous academic standards and our insistence that a college degree represent real achievement.

Or we can assume that society's obligation (and its own self-interest, as well) is to provide more than just the chance to walk through the college gate—that there must also be access to a useful and personally significant educational experience.

These two assumptions by no means exclude each other. Some dropouts, for example, are flunk-outs; some clearly are not, or need not be, within alternative teaching-learning formats. Some who drop out may indeed never have been "college material" in the first place. But in the absence of some specification of what is meant by "college," the question must be asked whether different and differing types of colleges would meet student needs more effectively than do the present forms. In the few examples we have found in which the college format has been adapted to meet the needs of a particular group of students who would normally have had a high attrition rate, strikingly lower dropout rates have resulted.[11] In a broader formulation, the question is really what kind of a total "system" of higher education this Nation wants.

3

FOOTNOTES

1. The Paradox of Access

1. *Digest of Educational Statistics 1970*, U.S. Department of Health, Education and Welfare, Office of Education, National Center for Educational Statistics, Washington, 1970, p. 49.

2. "School Enrollment: October 1969," *Current Population Reports*, U.S. Bureau of the Census, series P–20, no. 206 (October 5, 1970), table 1; *Digest of Educational Statistics, op. cit.*, p. 67; *Projections of Educational Statistics to 1977–78*, U.S. Department of Health, Education, and Welfare, Office of Education, National Center for Educational Statistics, Washington, 1969; Joseph Froomkin, *Aspirations, Enrollments and Resources*, U.S. Department of Health, Education, and Welfare, Office of Education, Office of Program Planning and Evaluation, Washington, 1970, p. 28.

3. *Digest of Educational Statistics, op. cit.*, table 102; *Opening Fall Enrollment in Higher Education 1969*, U.S. Department of Health, Education, and Welfare, Office of Education, National Center for Educational Statistics, Washington, 1970, table 4; "Enrollment by Highly Selective Private Universities, Fall 1969," *Higher Education General Information Survey*, U.S. Department of Health, Education, and Welfare, Office of Education, National Center for Educational Statistics, Washington.

4. *Digest of Educational Statistics, op. cit.*

5. *The Statistical Abstract of the United States, 1970*, 91st Annual Edition, U.S. Bureau of the Census, p. 104, table no. 147.

6. See, for example, the reports of the Carnegie Commission on Higher Education, Berkeley: *Quality and Equality: New Levels of Federal Responsibility for Higher Education—A Special Report and Recommendations by the Commission, December 1968; Quality and Equality: Revised Recommendations— A Supplement to the 1968 Special Report by the Commission*, June 1970; *A Chance to Learn: An Action Agenda for Equal Opportunity in Higher Education—A Special Report and Recommendations by the Commission*, March 1970, all published by McGraw-Hill, New York; also *Priorities in Higher Education, The Report of the President's Task Force on Higher Education* (Hester Commission), August 1970, U.S. Government Printing Office, Washington, D.C.; *The Federal Financing of Higher Education*, Association of American Universities, Washington, D.C., 1968; *The Federal Investment in Higher Education: Needed Next Steps*, American Council on Education, Washington, D.C. 1969; *The Federal Government and Higher Education*, Report of the Advisory Committee on Higher Education to the Secretary of Health, Education, and Welfare, Washington, D.C., 1968.

7. These are approximations derived in and from several different sources: Robert H. Berls, "Higher Education Opportunity and Achievement in the United States," *The Economics and Financing of Higher Education in the United States, A*

Compendium of Papers Submitted to the Joint Economic Committee of the Congress, 91st Congress, 1st Session, U.S. Government Printing Office, 1969; *Digest of Educational Statistics, op. cit.;* A. W. Astin, "Undergraduate Achievement and Institutional Excellence," *Science,* August 16, 1968, pp. 661–668; *Admission and Retention of Students,* Master Plan Phase III, Board of Higher Education, Springfield, Ill., 1969; James Trent and Leland Medsker, *Beyond High School,* San Francisco, 1968; *Phase I Final Report and Phase II Final Report,* Northern California Cooperative Research Project on Student Withdrawals (Norcal Project), 1969 and 1970, Thomas F. MacMillan, Project Director, Napa, Calif.; Bruce K. Ecklund, "College Dropouts Who Came Back," *Harvard Educational Review,* 1964, pp. 402–20; A. W. Astin and R. J. Panos, "Attrition Among College Students," *American Educational Research Journal,* January 1968, pp. 57–72; and data collected from a number of individual colleges. A nationwide profile of school attainment among a complete age cohort can be derived from "Educational Attainment, March 1970," *Current Population Reports,* U.S. Bureau of the Census, Series P-20, No. 207. The list of the 15 most selective institutions was derived from the American Council on Education Study, *An Assessment of Quality In Graduate Education,* prepared by Allan M. Cartter in 1966, as well as the most recent ACE study published in December of 1970. Even though these studies rated graduate education only, the presumption is that high standards of selectivity for undergraduate students would obtain as well.

The large State universities referred to are those whose single campuses, regardless of whether they were part of a State system, had 15,000 or more full-time enrolled students in the fall of 1969. These were obtained from table 4, *HEGIS Report IV 2.3,* U.S. Department of Health, Education, and Welfare, Office of Education, National Center for Educational Statistics, Washington, 1969.

8. Norman Pearlstine, "The University of Texas Works Hard to Improve, Yet the Past Lingers," *Wall Street Journal,* January 20, 1969.

9. *Five Years Later,* Division of Institutional Research, Office of the Chancellor, California State Colleges, Los Angeles, April 1970, pp. 13–14, and discussions with the Office of the Chancellor.

10. Academic failure is not the most common reason for "dropping out" of college. Alexander Astin and Robert Panos ("Attrition Among College Students," *American Educational Research Journal,* January 1968, p. 63) found that, for men, the major reasons for leaving were changing plans, dissatisfaction with college, finances, wanting time to reconsider interests and goals, and academic failure, in that order. For women, the five most important reasons for leaving college were marriage, dissatisfaction with the college environment, changing career plans, finances, and reconsideration of interests and goals, in that order of importance. Academic failure was eighth among major reasons for women to leave college. Dropping out is more a function of a poor fit between the nature of present institutions and the expectations and goals of present-day students. Other commonly cited reasons for students' dropping out, other than academic failure, are lack of interest in their studies, feelings of loneliness and isolation (at large institutions), becoming tired of being a student, and desire to travel or interrupt education.

Some people return to college after a period of absence, working, traveling, and reassessing their goals. Measurements of students "dropping back in" are difficult to obtain. Some students drop in and out several times. Some return after a short absence, some after a long absence. Some finish after returning, some do not. Many students, after leaving one institution, will enter another institution. There is no precise way to measure these ebbs and flows of the student attendance.

Measuring college dropouts is therefore difficult to do with any accuracy, especially when a variety of things is meant by the term "drop out." Another reason for the inaccuracy of the measurement is that students who leave college may be less than frank about the real reasons that caused them to leave. That is, perceived social pressure, peer-group consciousness, or personal reasons may affect the reporting of reasons for leaving, which will in turn lead to inaccurate tallies on reasons for failure to complete a college course in the standard 4-year term at one school.

The following bear on the problem of explaining dropout rates: Berls, *op. cit.;* Carnegie Commission on Higher Education, *Less Time, More Options,* Berkeley, December 1970; Amitai Etzioni and Murray Milner, *Higher Education in An Active Society,* Bureau of Social Science Research, Washington, 1970; *Admission and Retention of Students,* Master Plan, Phase III, Committee B, Illinois Board of Higher Education, Chicago, 1969.

11. The College for Human Services in New York City and Northeastern University in Boston are two excellent examples of this point.

APPENDIX B LETTERS FROM TWO STUDENTS

March 10, 1966

Dear Sirs:

Although three semesters have passed since I was a student on the University's campus, I have never forgotten any part of my life there.

While there, I made a lot of foolish and childish mistakes. As a result, I can't say that it was the fault of being in such an anonymous atmosphere or having counselors who were never interested enough, that caused my failure. I do hope that with the lapse of time between now and then, I can present to you some valid and fairly objective reasons behind my failure that will assist you in your survey.

As an only child, I was never bothered with other people running into my room or with being confronted with the temptation to take a long coffee break. Being away from home for the first time presented many temptations. Of course, I had always been told that the friends made in college are the ones who stand by for a life-time. Being immersed in such an atmosphere where I was exposed to so many new faces, I had the desire to feel important; to have some significance, and to develop some genuine friendships. Family background, color and religion meant nothing to me during that first year. Each student was at the University because of his ability; therefore, everyone was equal. Unfortunately though, I could never distinguish between the true friend and the merely superficial one. I always felt that having friends (the number never mattered) was just as important to my happiness as academic success. As a result, when I did face scholastic problems, I sought companionship and confidence in friendships. The problem was that I could never balance my friends with my academic responsibilities.

Throughout my first semester, I realized that I was having more problems than I had ever experienced in high school. But I thought that this was to be expected. It was unfortunate that my high school instructors and counselors, as well as the speakers during Orientation made the

University appear as such a rigorous school. So many adults who have had contact with the University had commented that freshmen should be satisfied with "C's". Even before I started classes, my goals had been completely lowered. Everyone, including the administrator who stood on stage to say that one out of every three would not return for his sophomore year, had gradually caused me to view "A's" and "B's" as intangible. As a result, there was no striving for anything above a "C". I saw the University as a mongrel land of the survival of the fittest. I was sure that I could survive even if I didn't get the best grades. This did not mean that I was apathetic; I had merely accepted the fact that I would not receive grades equal to what I had earned in high school.

I think that it is a great mistake of school officials to attach so much difficulty with the first year on campus. Perhaps such warnings are good, in that they show the student that he shouldn't expect an easy road, but they are also a source of great discouragement.

I have always blamed a part of my failing on my high school education. Nevertheless, I have always wondered why my high school counselors continued to "warn" everyone about the University. If the high school had provided an adequate amount of instruction, would there be any need to continue telling the student to be apprehensive. I had always thought that while there would be some difficult adjustments to make upon entering college, the learning process would be a fairly smooth and gradual transition. Instead, the contrast of high school and college was incongruent and alarming. Very little that I had learned in high school was helpful during my first year because I had not had enough high school preparation to connect anything with the college courses. My social science courses in high school taught me about the workings of government and economics, but the only necessity was to memorize the printed page and rewrite those facts on a test. Because I had been conditioned to this for four years, I could not learn quickly enough to re-adjust my study patterns. I could not apply any of my previous study methods. Facts were relevant to the courses, but they were not the central requirement. My high school training had been deficient, and as a result, I had so many questions concerning the things that I didn't understand, that I was almost ashamed to ask too many questions in class. Because of such an anonymous feeling in the lecture room, I was not inclined to go to my instructors for assistance. Instead, I continued to feel lost and defeated.

At the close of the first semester, I was one honor point below a 2.0. and was placed on academic probation. Although this caused a stronger defeatist attitude, I had some feeling that the worst could never happen. I had had so much success in high school that I was confident that I could never be dismissed from the University. Nevertheless, I was. Although this seemed like a fatal blow to me at the time, I have learned since then that my debacle did have a definite purpose.

The following fall, I attended another state university. I thought that I had learned from past mistakes so that I would have no more problems in personal or academic adjustment. However, at the end of the semester, I realized that I had not been successful. I could find no contentment and no satisfaction in myself or in college life. From February, 1965 until the following September, I did nothing. I had just given up on a college education because I had lost all confidence. Living in a small town, I could find no employment. I just saw myself as entirely futile and without purpose.

Although those seven months were filled with despair and self-pity, I found that I did little else except think about my education. Certainly without it, I was suffering, and I knew that unless I became determined not to give up, I would continue suffering for a great many years.

Through the Extension Service of the University I have learned a great deal. There are so many factors on a college campus that cannot be helped; they are an accepted part of campus life. But it was not until I lost all exposure to the campus that I began to shape and formulate my own beliefs, ideas and ideals for the first time.

Last fall, I was very apprehensive about commuting. I thought that perhaps living at home would be very stifling. I was afraid that I would have no freedom of thought but would constantly be under my parents' surveillance. I am very pleased to admit that I was mistaken. Living away from the campus, I find that I have done something about cultivation of the individual.

Several weeks ago, I visited some friends on campus and was displeased to find that in spite of their educations, they conform to nothing but campus morals and ethics. No one seemed able to think on his own. Every comment made was based on an idea or a belief of another member of their peer group. I realize that this does not provide a fair representation of the student body, but these people are juniors and seniors. They have changed little since they entered as freshmen and were always under the influence of older students.

Because I haven't been a part of this student body for so long, I realize that I really don't have the right to underestimate the individualism which is being formed in these people. In comparing my life to theirs, however, I would say that because these students are always in a competitive environment, their courses are staying only within the lecture room and on the bluebook. They are taking none of the philosophies learned to see whether or not they agree. A grade is the only objective in the course; after that course is taken, nothing remains imprinted in the student's mind.

I remember that while I was on campus, there was an editorial in the *Daily* concerning the reasons for grades. We do need them, but why do they have to be the only thing? While commuting, I have found that not being exposed to the college atmosphere has made studying much more rewarding because I want to learn something and transfer it to my own life and philosophies. I am not studying merely because I realize that the closed door across the hall indicates that another student is studying for the same course to try to get a better grade than I.

One of the main reasons for my academic problems lies in the distribution courses. I am majoring in English Literature and am minoring in Speech. The purpose of the liberal arts school is to give a broad knowledge, but why must an English major begin with two and three hour courses in his major and four and five hour courses in the natural and social science fields? While I can do well—"A's" and "B's" in my fields of interest—I find that in the regular academic load, these grades mean little when evaluated with the four-hour courses in which I do poorly. It is interesting to explore other fields, but with the twelve and fourteen hour requirements of the social and natural science courses, how can one learn or retain enough to have an adequate knowledge of anything after graduation?

Also, if these courses must be taught, why do they have to have such a heavy bearing on the final academic average? It would be better for the student to have the distribution requirements figured separately from the courses of his concentration. If this were not feasible, perhaps there could be some program of grading that would not mean destruction if the student were not so successful in the general requirements.

My purpose in learning is to become a specialist in a given field. Once I graduate, I will not profess to know anything about political science or physiological psychology. One of my instructors summed this up well when she said, "You can't teach a fish to fly and you can't teach a hawk to swim." Meanwhile, liberal arts colleges persist in trying.

It is unfortunate that the freshman is exposed to so many teaching fellows. When I saw these people standing in front of the class, it created an uncomfortable feeling. Because most of them were only a few years older than the students, I always felt that they would never understand how anyone could have problems in a course in which they had so much interest. There was always an impenetrable wall between the instructor and myself. It was not until last semester that this wall was dissolved. For the first time, I encountered instructors who had been in the teaching profession for many years and who had received their doctorates. These people were genuinely devoted to their students. I respected each one so much for his knowledge and his interest. Because each was older, I felt that he was much wiser and much more understanding. I will always be grateful to these faculty members because they helped me so very much.

In order to do well in a course, a student has to know that there is a rapport between himself and his instructor. Through such intense interest that these instructors showed me, there came an added stimulus to do well. With this came another stimulus. After I receive my degree, I want to continue my education in the field of counseling. Because of my past academic problems, I suddenly feel what might be termed a "calling" to this profession. I know that an instructor is of little avail after a student has failed. If he shows interest and concern for the student from the first day that he enters the classroom, problems might be avoided.

I feel that because of my past failures, I perhaps have gained a little more insight into students than the students who have comfortably drifted through on "3.0's". There is so much more to a student's grade problems than his difficulties with a particular course. An instructor should realize that every student with difficulties is more than an automaton who enters class and leaves it again. He is also a human being, and the instructor must accept him with his human emotions and frailties. I will always remember one of my counselors sending a girl back to her dormitory because she was crying. When she left, his comment was that a student has to remember that when she comes to see an instructor, it's just not in good taste to cry. My first impulse was to think that in other words, it just wasn't "in good taste" to be human.

I only hope that through my past failings, I have learned not only how to take courses, but also how to accept life. Last semester, I abolished the lackadaisical attitude of being just an average student. The result of the semester was an "A" in each course. This did a great deal for me, but I will never forget that I am fallible. I have no bitterness towards undergraduate education, but I do believe that every administrator, instructor and student should evaluate his purposes and his practice honestly and clearly. If each would come half-way to meet the other, a great many of the undergraduate turmoils could be avoided.

When I petitioned to the Board at the University, I commented that I knew the meaning of the adage, "God teaches not by ideas, but by mistakes and contradictions." As I look back, I can see that I knew very little of its significance. Now, I am beginning to understand the true value of its connotation as it is applied to education and to life.

Yours very truly,

Cynthia

Note. In 1974 Cynthia was working as an insurance underwriter with a national insurance company, her second professional position. After earning her baccalaureate degree, she followed her "calling," becoming a program director for student activities at a state university. This letter is printed here with her permission. The identity of the university has been obscured.

March 14, 1966

Dear Mr. Cope:

It was rather ironic that when I started this letter I should receive another questionnaire from you concerning the survey. I realize the survey is important, although I doubt that one less form would make any big hole in the results. You also mentioned that all questionnaires are confidential, well I am not concerned in the least whether what I am writing to you is confidential or not. In fact I would enjoy sending a duplicate of this letter to the President of the University, although it would not accomplish anything except my own satisfaction.

I did not want to just fill out the form you sent me because in all honesty, I do not feel any of the questions are relevant to my withdrawal from the University. So I felt it would be more beneficial for me and possibly for your survey if I enclose a letter to you explaining the events leading up to my "withdrawal" and why.

I started attending the University in the Fall of 1962. I was planning upon majoring in elementary education, but as you are aware, all such students must first complete the requirements of the first two years of Literature, Arts & Science School. My second semester, I was carrying all courses which were hard for me, particularly science and language, and no matter how hard I studied, which I did all the time, I still received final grades of C's. In this semester, I took Astronomy and received a D because I was too honest to listen to the other students and would not cheat on exams, for which I will never be sorry. With this D, I was placed on probation in the Fall of 1963.

During the summer of 1963, I attended summer school and also my mother had a serious operation at which time it was discovered she had cancer. So with going to school, caring for my mother, and our home, come September, I was ready for a vacation which of course was not possible. Along with this, I was carrying my hardest subjects, which at the end of the term would have completed my requirements for LSA school and then I would be free to start study in my field of interest, education.

In this Fall semester '63, I was taking a course which my "counselor" had advised me to take. It was a Psychology course and over 75% of the students were seniors and graduate students. If my counselor had known anything at all about advising, which few seem to he would never have advised such a course to a sophomore on probation. I even went to him, within the legal time period, and requested to drop it, but he said, "Give it a try." Maybe this was *one* of the means to "weed-out" students, I do not know. I did receive my second D, Psychology, and although I had a high B on the Astronomy 112 final examination, I received a C+ rather than a B– which would have made all the difference in my average. Therefore because of two D's, I was requested to withdraw for I had not met the terms of the probation period.

I was told I could appeal my case *in person* to the Probation Board, but this was not allowed for some reason unknown to me. So I submitted a letter to the Board, December 1963, stating my reasons for why I felt I had performed as I had; reasons stated earlier in this letter. My father, who is a University graduate, and I both went up to the University and spoke with the Dean, whom I contacted when I felt my advisor could not help me. The Dean informed us that my letter, which had been submitted the day before, had been turned down by the Board, and I could not be given another chance. The reason the Board had decided such, the Dean said, was not because I had received two D's, for the Board did feel my reasons for poor performance were sound ones and I was willing to try, but they had to turn me down because of the SAT scores and other tests used for this purpose. The Dean agreed because my score was not at the University's usual level that I could not be given another chance. This I do not understand (the reasoning behind his statement) for a friend of mine was in the same situation, and this person was given two chances. Also several others I know, and have proof of have been on academic probation for three or four times in a row and still are attending. So the only conclusion I can come to is the University cares more for "scores" in students than for those people who may have to work a little harder and may not receive all A's but in the end benefit far more from their education than those who can brag of high "scores".

I feel today the University cares only about seeing how large a student body it can acquire in competition with other universities. And it makes me shutter [sic] to see students treated like machines. I am well aware of the fact that schools are overcrowded, but I also know that if a college cannot handle adequately and fairly such a large number of students, then it is a big mistake on the college's part to enroll numbers it cannot care for.

The question I ask myself is if the administration is so concerned about the welfare of its students, why then are there so many incidents occuring on campus of mental breakdowns, suicides, cheating, and such! You may think I am being silly, but I feel the problems of the students are important and someone somewhere needs to be concerned in our colleges with this problem.

From this letter you may feel I am very bitter towards the University. No, not the University, only the rules that apply to some and not others, and at the administrators who set standards which are for some students and not for others. I just wish I knew where they draw their line or else what kind of pull some students have that allow "special cases".

While I was at the University, I loved every minute and if it were not for realizing this school is not noted for its Education School, I would be back in a minute, that is if the University would consider a B average from a "lesser college" of any value. The University still holds a very special meaning for me and I am just sorry to see what is happening to it today.

I am sorry, Mr. Cope, that I do not feel I can answer your questionnaire, but I would not be honest with you or myself if I did so. I do hope I have not slowed up your survey too much, although I am more than sure my slowness has had no serious effect. I had intended upon answering it immediately but with going to school, running our home, and caring for my mother, who passed away February 8, I have just no had time to sit down and write this letter till now. I am truly sorry.

Please feel free to show this letter to whomever you wish. I am not worried about it being confidential. Also if there is any other information you may need, please feel free to contact me and I promise to respond immediately.

Sincerely,

Catherine

Note. Catherine received her degree and teaching certificate in 1967. After teaching for several years, she "retired" to raise a family. Her plans in 1974 are to eventually return to teaching. This letter is printed with her permission. It has been changed slightly to avoid identifying the University and to avoid mentioning specific individuals.

APPENDIX C   THE RELATIONSHIP OF
BIPOLAR PERSONALITY TRAITS
AND ENVIRONMENTAL PRESSES

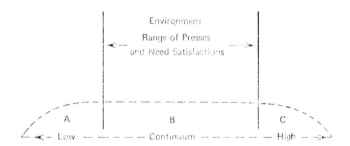

The range of the environment's presses and need satisfactions are represented by the vertical lines. The curved line represents the assumed greater diversity of student personality traits. Students with traits in the "A" or "C" areas tend to be less congruent with the environment. In terms of self-selection out or selective expulsion it seems that these means of selection may operate differently depending on the press and personality trait being considered. For example, in an institution of higher education there is an academic press-ability continuum. The academic press may mean in the "A" area there will be both selective expulsion (academic dismissal) *and* self-selection out ("I had better transfer somewhere else where it is easier, where I can handle the work"). However, at the "C" end of the academic continuum, where the student has more than enough ability, there is only self-selection out of the institution.

When considering a social press such as "cosmopolitanism," the students who are not congruent at either the "A" or "C" ends of the continuum may elect to leave the institution (self-selection out), but for different reasons. Those students who are less cosmopolitan (i.e., more provincial, less worldly) may tend to find the social (and academic) environment threatening, overwhelming, and otherwise unsettling. The most cosmopolitan student may, however, find that he is not challenged or stimulated in this setting and will likewise leave.

Thus, while incongruence may, in this example, be present in two areas, the nature of the behavior and the type of mechanism for selection differs depending on the press and personality trait under consideration.

APPENDIX D INSTITUTIONAL CLASSIFICATION SHEET (IC)

INSTITUTIONAL CLASSIFICATION SHEET (IC)

PROJECT ON STUDENT DEVELOPMENT IN SMALL COLLEGES

STUDY OF ATTRITION   CLASSIFICATION OF DROP-OUTS

Student Name_____ _____ _____ Date_____
                    Last   Initial   First

Student Address_____ _____ _____
                    Street & No.   City   State & Zip

Parents' Name_____

Parents' Address_____ _____ _____
                    Street & No.   City   State & Zip

- -

Code No._____ Age_____ Sex_____ Date of Withdrawal_____

SAT Scores V____ M____ ACT Score-Composite_____ H.S. GPA_____ % H.S. Rank_____

The following classifications should be used in supplying the Project Office with
information concerning this study of student attrition.

FOR *ALL* STUDENTS WHO WITHDRAW PLEASE PROVIDE APPROPRIATE INFORMATION FOR SECTIONS
A, B, AND C.

> Section A   CIRCLE *SINGLE* MOST APPROPRIATE NUMBER
>
> 1.1 Involuntary withdrawal
> 1.2 Voluntary withdrawal
>
>
> Section B   CIRCLE *SINGLE* MOST APPROPRIATE NUMBER
>
> 2.1 Academic performance inadequate; grade point average
>   required discontinuance
> 2.2 Academic performance marginal; on academic probation
> 2.3 Academic performance adequate
>
>
> Section C   CIRCLE *SINGLE* MOST APPROPRIATE NUMBER
>
> 3.1 Behavior and relationships with college authorities
>   required discontinuance
> 3.2 Behavior and relationships with college authorities
>   troublesome, but did not require discontinuation
> 3.3 No difficulties in behavior or relationships with college

152

FOR *EACH* STUDENT FOR WHOM INFORMATION IS AVAILABLE, COMPLETE NEXT TWO SECTIONS.

Section D   CIRCLE *SINGLE* MOST APPROPRIATE NUMBER

    4.1 Expecting to return
    4.2 Not expecting to return
    4.3 Undetermined or unknown

Section E   CIRCLE *SINGLE* MOST APPROPRIATE NUMBER

    5.1 Left to transfer to another educational institution
    5.2 Left to go to work
    5.3 Left to travel
    5.4 Left for military service
    5.5 Left with no explicit plans
    5.6 None of these

Section F   CIRCLE MOST APPROPRIATE NUMBER OPPOSITE *EACH* ITEM TO
                INDICATE DEGREE OF IMPORTANCE

None	Minimum	Moderate	Major	
6.0	6.1	6.2	6.3	Financial Need
7.0	7.1	7.2	7.3	Personal Illness
8.0	8.1	8.2	8.3	Family Illness
9.0	9.1	9.2	9.3	Emotional and/or Social Difficulties
10.0	10.1	10.2	10.3	Differing Goals, Values, Interests
11.0	11.1	11.2	11.3	Had no clear educational objectives
12.0	12.1	12.2	12.3	Marriage
13.0	13.1	13.2	13.3	Pregnancy
14.0	14.1	14.2	14.3	Parents desired withdrawal
15.0	15.1	15.2	15.3	Drafted--armed services
16.0	16.1	16.2	16.3	Other--specify:_____

Section G   CIRCLE MOST APPROPRIATE NUMBER OPPOSITE *EACH* ITEM TO
                INDICATE DEGREE OF IMPORTANCE

None	Minimum	Moderate	Major	
17.0	17.1	17.2	17.3	College did not offer program needed
18.0	18.1	18.2	18.3	College work too difficult
19.0	19.1	19.2	19.3	Felt out of place
20.0	20.1	20.2	20.3	Dissatisfied with faculty and/or in-stitution
21.0	21.1	21.2	21.3	Too much emphasis on religion
22.0	22.1	22.2	22.3	Too many rules; too much supervision
23.0	23.1	23.2	23.3	Too much freedom
24.0	24.1	24.2	24.3	Other--specify:_____

Add here additional information significant for this student_____
_____
_____

APPENDIX E STUDENT QUESTIONNAIRE (SQ)

STUDENT QUESTIONNAIRE (SQ)

PROJECT ON STUDENT DEVELOPMENT IN SMALL COLLEGES
COUNCIL FOR THE ADVANCEMENT OF SMALL COLLEGES
Administrative Offices
Plainfield, Vermont

ATTRITION STUDY QUESTIONNAIRE

This questionnaire attempts to provide a framework within which you can give the information mentioned in our letter. You will notice that alternatives have been provided for you to rank or check. In addition, often we have provided space where you can write in statements of your own. We provide this space because we recognize that the alternatives given may well not cover adequately all circumstances and that in some instances you may wish to use your own words as well as checking one of the alternatives. You should feel free, therefore, to check or rank where that response most nearly describes your own situation and to add your own comments where you feel clarification is necessary. Our aim is to provide a context in which you can present your own situation as accurately and easily as possible.

Please return the completed questionnaire directly to us in the enclosed stamped envelope. If you have any questions, feel free to write. If you would like to receive copies of reports growing out of this study, please so indicate on the last page of this questionnaire.

Code Number .... Please Check: Male ...... Female ......

Our first area of concern is why you left and the circumstances at the time.

CIRCLE **SINGLE** MOST APPROPRIATE NUMBER IN **EACH SECTION.**

SECTION A

    1.1 I left involuntarily
    1.2 I left voluntarily

SECTION B

    2.1 My academic performance was inadequate; grade point average required discontinuance.
    2.2 My academic performance was marginal; on academic probation.
    2.3 My academic performance was adequate or better.

SECTION C

    3.1 My behavior and relationships with college authorities required discontinuance.
    3.2 My behavior and relationships with college authorities troublesome, but did not require discontinuation.
    3.3 I had no difficulties in behavior or relationships with college.

SECTION D

    4.1 I left expecting to return
    4.2 I left not expecting to return
    4.3 I left uncertain about returning

SECTION E

    5.1 I left intending to transfer to another educational institution
    5.2 I left intending to go to work
    5.3 I left intending to travel
    5.4 I left intending to enter military service
    5.5 I left with no explicit plans
    5.6 None of these

SECTION F   CIRCLE MOST APPROPRIATE NUMBER OPPOSITE **EACH ITEM** IN SECTIONS F, G, AND
H TO INDICATE THE IMPORTANCE OF EACH FACTOR TO YOUR DECISION.

None	Minimum	Moderate	Major	
6.0	6.1	6.2	6.3	Financial Need
7.0	7.1	7.2	7.3	Personal Illness
8.0	8.1	8.2	8.3	Family Illness
9.0	9.1	9.2	9.3	Emotional and/or Social Difficulties
10.0	10.1	10.2	10.3	Goals, Values, Interests Different from College
11.0	11.1	11.2	11.3	Had No Clear Educational Objectives
12.0	12.1	12.2	12.3	Marriage
13.0	13.1	13.2	13.3	Pregnancy
14.0	14.1	14.2	14.3	Parents Desired Withdrawal
15.0	15.1	15.2	15.3	Drafted — Armed Forces
16.0	16.1	16.2	16.3	Other (Please describe) ....

SECTION G

None	Minimum	Moderate	Major	
17.0	17.1	17.2	17.3	College did not offer program needed
18.0	18.1	18.2	18.3	College work too difficult
19.0	19.1	19.2	19.3	Felt out of place
20.0	20.1	20.2	20.3	Dissatisfied with faculty and/or institution
21.0	21.1	21.2	21.3	Too much emphasis on religion
22.0	22.1	22.2	22.3	Too many rules; too much supervision
23.0	23.1	23.2	23.3	Too much freedom
24.0	24.1	24.2	24.3	Other (Please describe) ....

Add here any additional significant information ....

....

SECTION H

None	Minimum	Moderate	Major	
25.0	25.1	25.2	25.3	Academic underachievement or difficulty
26.0	26.1	26.2	26.3	Argument with friend of opposite sex
27.0	27.1	27.2	27.3	Argument with friend of same sex
28.0	28.1	28.2	28.3	Discrepancy between college professed beliefs and actual behavior
29.0	29.1	29.2	29.3	Conflict with college authorities
30.0	30.1	30.2	30.3	Disliked general atmosphere and activities
31.0	31.1	31.2	31.3	Had chance for a good job
32.0	32.1	32.2	32.3	Wanted to get married
33.0	33.1	33.2	33.3	Heard about another school that seemed better
34.0	34.1	34.2	34.3	Forced to decide on major or life's work before ready
35.0	35.1	35.2	35.3	Unreasonable parental standards
36.0	36.1	36.2	36.3	None of the above, I just felt uncomfortable
37.0	37.1	37.2	37.3	Other (Please describe) ....

Write the number of the reason above which first provoked you to think of leaving ....

Secondary reason ....

Our next concern is with issues related to time of leaving.

COMPLETE EACH SECTION (I through K)

SECTION I

1. I first thought of leaving even before entering college.   Yes ....   No ....
2. After entering, I first thought I might leave the college in the first ..... second ..... third .....
   fourth ..... fifth ..... sixth ..... seventh ..... semester.
3. If possible, name the month in the particular semester ....

SECTION J

1. I finally left college in: Month ....   Year ....
2. College was ...... was not ...... in session.

SECTION K

1. How long did you remain in school after first thinking of leaving? .... (Please write number
   of weeks)

CIRCLE **SINGLE** MOST APPROPRIATE NUMBER IN **EACH SECTION** (L through O)

SECTION L

After leaving college I lived —
1. At home (parent's)
2. At another college
3. In military quarters
4. In my own apartment, room, or house
   (alone, with friend(s))
5. Other ....

SECTION M

I am currently living —
1. At home (parent's)
2. At another college
3. In military quarters
4. In my own apartment, room, or house
   (alone, with friend(s))
5. Other ....

SECTION N

Upon leaving college —
1. I went to work
2. I traveled around for a while
3. I loafed around for a while
4. I went to school
5. I stayed home and studied
6. I married
7. I went into military service

SECTION O

I am currently —
1. Working
2. Traveling
3. Unemployed
4. At another college
5. Studying on my own at home
6. Married
7. In military service

Please add here any significant information about where you have been and what you have been doing
since leaving college.

....
....
....
....
....

Next, we would like to know with whom you discussed the decision and what was talked about as the decision was considered.

SECTION P

Listed down the page are various topics which may have come up for discussion. Across the page are listed various persons with whom you may have discussed these topics. Please indicate the topics which were discussed and the persons with whom they were discussed by CIRCLING THE APPROPRIATE NUMBER(S) OPPOSITE EACH TOPIC. Leave blank any topics not discussed.

	Friend of the same sex	Friend of opposite sex	Father	Mother	Brother or sister	Teacher on faculty	Dean or administrator	College Counselor	Psychologist - Psychiatrist	Pastor	Other (Specify)
Academic underachievement / difficulty	0	1	2	3	4	5	6	7	8	9	10
Problems with friend of opposite sex	0	1	2	3	4	5	6	7	8	9	10
Problems with friend of same sex	0	1	2	3	4	5	6	7	8	9	10
Difficulty with peers in general	0	1	2	3	4	5	6	7	8	9	10
Difficulty with faculty member(s)	0	1	2	3	4	5	6	7	8	9	10
Problems with college authorities	0	1	2	3	4	5	6	7	8	9	10
Problems with parents	0	1	2	3	4	5	6	7	8	9	10
Financial problems	0	1	2	3	4	5	6	7	8	9	10
Religious beliefs	0	1	2	3	4	5	6	7	8	9	10
Attitudes and values	0	1	2	3	4	5	6	7	8	9	10
Educational plans and purposes	0	1	2	3	4	5	6	7	8	9	10
Vocational plans	0	1	2	3	4	5	6	7	8	9	10
Plans concerning life in general	0	1	2	3	4	5	6	7	8	9	10
College rules and regulations	0	1	2	3	4	5	6	7	8	9	10
Limitations in college curriculum	0	1	2	3	4	5	6	7	8	9	10
Limitations in extra-curricular opportunities	0	1	2	3	4	5	6	7	8	9	10
Marriage	0	1	2	3	4	5	6	7	8	9	10
Pregnancy	0	1	2	3	4	5	6	7	8	9	10
Educational opportunities elsewhere	0	1	2	3	4	5	6	7	8	9	10
Job opportunities elsewhere	0	1	2	3	4	5	6	7	8	9	10

Please circle two numbers to indicate with whom most significant discussions were held;

0   1   2   3   4   5   6   7   8   9   10

Which of the above persons did you speak to first ..... (write number) second ..... third ..... fourth ..... fifth ......?

What actions by others might have made a difference in your decision to withdraw? ....

....

....

....

What finally crystallized your decision to withdraw? ....

....

....

SECTION Q

Please indicate which feelings you experienced and how strongly they were felt by CIRCLING THE APPROPRIATE NUMBER OPPOSITE **EACH FEELING** DESCRIBED below.

	I Did Not Have This Feeling	I Felt This Only Slightly	I Felt This Strongly	This Was One of My Strongest Feelings
Happy about future plans	0	1	2	3
Uncertain about future plans	0	1	2	3
Relieved to be leaving	0	1	2	3
Unhappy about leaving	0	1	2	3
Disappointed in myself	0	1	2	3
Uncertain about my abilities	0	1	2	3
Confident about performance in future situations	0	1	2	3
Unconcerned	0	1	2	3
Anxious	0	1	2	3
Confident about my decision	0	1	2	3
Uncertain about my decision	0	1	2	3
Angry at college	0	1	2	3
Angry at society of which college is a part	0	1	2	3
Angry at parents	0	1	2	3
Angry at myself	0	1	2	3
Disillusioned with colleges in general	0	1	2	3
Other (Please describe)	0	1	2	3

Our next concern is with your feelings in relation to leaving or while you were considering whether or not to leave.

SECTION R

Listed down the page are various actions and responses which might have occurred, and across the page are listed persons who may have offered them. Please indicate the actions and responses you experienced and the persons with whom they were encountered by CIRCLING THE APPROPRIATE NUMBERS. Leave blank any actions or responses you did not encounter.

	Friend of the same sex	Friend of opposite sex	Father	Mother	Brother or sister	Teacher on faculty	Dean or administrator	College Counselor	Psychologist - Psychiatrist	Pastor	Other (Specify)
Urged me to remain	0	1	2	3	4	5	6	7	8	9	10
Urged me to leave	0	1	2	3	4	5	6	7	8	9	10
Mainly interested in the welfare of the college	0	1	2	3	4	5	6	7	8	9	10
Felt I had failed	0	1	2	3	4	5	6	7	8	9	10
Uninterested — did not really care	0	1	2	3	4	5	6	7	8	9	10
Objectively tried to help me consider pros and cons	0	1	2	3	4	5	6	7	8	9	10
Was warm and understanding	0	1	2	3	4	5	6	7	8	9	10
Did not understand	0	1	2	3	4	5	6	7	8	9	10
Understanding but disappointed	0	1	2	3	4	5	6	7	8	9	10
Other (Describe)	0	1	2	3	4	5	6	7	8	9	10

Finally we would like to have your overall reactions to your withdrawal and to your college experience.

SECTION S

In the light of what has happened since, in what ways was your withdrawal wise or unwise?

....
....
....
....
....
....
....
....

What are some specific results, either positive or negative, of your experience at the college?

....
....
....
....
....
....
....

I would .... would not .... like to receive copies of reports of this research.

APPENDIX F EXAMPLES OF FOLLOW-UP QUESTIONNAIRES[1]

BERKELEY

Office of Institutional Research

To the College Student
Please complete this questionnaire to the best of your ability. Read each question carefully and indicate your considered answer where appropriate.

1. Please indicate whether either of the following statements applies to you:

Check here if this statement ap-   ☐   I did not register at the Univer-
plies to you   sity Fall Quarter of 1975 as I
                                           planned to take the quarter off;
                                           however, I am continuing my
                                           studies at the University and
                                           have registered for Winter
                                           Quarter, 1976.

Check here if this statement ap-   ☐   I received a degree from the
plies to you   University at the end of the
                                           Spring or Summer Quarter of
                                           1975 and did not register for
                                           the Fall Quarter as I did not
                                           wish to seek another University
                                           degree at that time.

---

[1]Adapted from University of California, Berkeley, 1968 survey (ED 669 220), a report by Eleanor Langlois, *Graduate Attrition at Berkeley*, August 1972.

Note. If you check either of the above statements, you need not complete the remainder of this questionnaire. If you checked neither statement, please continue with the questionnaire.

Please enter your name here (regardless of whether or not you complete the remainder of the questionnaire):

Family Name	First and Middle Names

2. Please indicate by a check mark in the appropriate space whether each of the reasons listed below influenced your decision not to register at the University for the Fall Quarter of 1975.

Reason for not registering during the Fall Quarter of 1975	Influenced my decision	Did *not* influence my decision
a. Enrolled at another institution	_____	_____
b. Personal illness	_____	_____
c. Illness of another person	_____	_____
d. Voluntary military service	_____	_____
e. Involuntary military service	_____	_____
f. Expected to be drafted into military service	_____	_____
g. Sought full-time employment	_____	_____
h. Lacked funds to continue formal education	_____	_____
i. Marriage	_____	_____
j. Pregnancy or birth	_____	_____
k. Continued studies toward degree in a nonregistered status	_____	_____
l. Dissatisfaction with the program	_____	_____
m. Other, please specify	_____	_____

3. From the above list please select the *one reason that most*

influenced your decision not to register at the University for the Fall Quarter of 1975, and enter the letter preceding it in this space_____.

4. Please answer the following questions as appropriate:
   1. If you enrolled at another institution instead of registering at the University for the Fall Quarter of 1975, at which institution did you enroll?

   _____

   Please indicate briefly your reason for enrolling at another institution.

   _____
   _____
   _____

   2. If you enlisted in military service instead of registering at the University for the Fall Quarter of 1975, did you do this as an alternative to being drafted?

   Yes_____   No_____

   3. If you sought full-time employment instead of registering at the University for the Fall Quarter of 1975, did you intend this to be a temporary interruption of your studies?

   Yes_____   No_____

   4. If a lack of funds influenced your decision not to register at the University for the Fall Quarter of 1975, please check below the reason or reasons responsible for changing your financial support level.

   ____(a)   an increase in university fees

   ____(b)   unavailability of a grant, fellowship, assistantship, etc.

   ____(c)   unavailability of employment with salary adequate to needs.

   ____(d)   reduction of family (spouse, parents, etc.) support.

_____(e) offer of better financial support from another institution.

_____(f) other, please specify _____

SAN DIEGO

UNIVERSITY OF CALIFORNIA, SAN DIEGO

BERKELEY · DAVIS · IRVINE · LOS ANGELES · RIVERSIDE · SAN DIEGO · SAN FRANCISCO SANTA BARBARA · SANTA CRUZ

CHARLES J. HITCH
President of the University

WILLIAM D. McELROY
Chancellor at San Diego

OFFICE OF THE VICE CHANCELLOR-ACADEMIC AFFAIRS
LA JOLLA, CALIFORNIA 92037

Dear Student,

I have noted with regret that you have chosen to discontinue your educational program at UCSD. It is important to me and to the University to understand your personal reasons for not continuing your education here.

Please assist UCSD to better serve its students. Take a few minutes to complete the enclosed questionnaire, fold and fasten it, and drop it in the mail.

Sincerely,

Paul D. Saltman

		Please circle Yes, No, or
YOUR NAME _____		Doesn't Apply:

1. I have moved (plan to move) to another city in California . . . Y N DA

2. I like____, dislike____ San Diego/La Jolla as a residence
community . . . . Y N DA

3. I have moved or plan to move to another state . . . . Y N DA

4. I left UCSD because I lacked funds to continue my formal
education . . . . Y N DA

      Family support to me was reduced . . . . Y N DA

      I lost my part-time earnings . . . . Y N DA

      Financial aid I received was not adequate . . . . Y N DA

5. I left college to seek (accept) full-time employment . . . . . . Y N DA

6. I left college because I was losing interest in my studies . . . . . Y N DA

7. I left college because I wanted a vacation from schooling . . . . Y N DA

8. I left college because I wanted to travel . . . . Y N DA

9. I left college because of a change in marital status . . . . Y N DA

10. I left college because of illness . . . . Y N DA

      My own _____ That of a family member_____

11. I left college because of emotional discouragement . . . . Y N DA

12. I left UCSD because I became disenchanted with the goals and
values of higher education . . . . Y N DA

13. I left college because of excessive academic pressure . . . . . . Y N DA

14. I left college for personal reasons having nothing to do with UCSD,
its environment, or its location . . . . Y N DA

15. I left UCSD because of a change in my academic interests or
career objectives . . . . Y N DA

      Comment:

16. I left UCSD because I wished to transfer to another
college/university . . . . Y N DA

      Which one?_____

      Because it is smaller____ , larger____ than UCSD

      Because it has for me a more satisfying academic program____

      Because it may be more intellectually challenging _____

      Because it is less expensive to attend _____

      Because there would be less academic pressure _____

      Because it is farther away from my home town_____

      Because my husband/wife (boyfriend/girlfriend) is
      enrolled there _____

      Other_____

17. I plan to return to UCSD . . . . Y N DA

164

18. I left UCSD because I was disappointed:

    a.   In the courses offered . . . .   Y   N   DA

    b.   In the majors offered . . . .   Y   N   DA

    c.   In the size of classes. . . . .   Y   N   DA

    d.   In my instructors . . . .   Y   N   DA

    e.   In the social environment or social life . . . .   Y   N   DA

    f.   In the organized extracurricular activities . . . . . .   Y   N   DA

    g.   Other _____   Y   N   DA

    If one or more of choices (a) through (f), is significant to you,
    please elaborate here:

19. There are many times during a college career when you decide on your needs and
interests, and make choices in what to do. At these times various people may be
available to advise you or help you make up your mind. Please indicate below your
experience in each of these areas. If any experience was particularly good or bad,
or was influential in your decision to leave UCSD, a written comment would be
very useful. This will enable UCSD to improve the help that is available to students.

	If you didn't get help from this source:		If you did get help from this source, it was:				
	Didn't need it:	Wish I had had it:	USEFUL ◄Very Not at all►				
Counseling in high school as to what you want and can accomplish . . .	_____	_____	4	3	2	1	0
Information about what to expect at UCSD	_____	_____	4	3	2	1	0
Advice at freshman registration about course choices	_____	_____	4	3	2	1	0
Counseling to help you plan a satisfying major or career	_____	_____	4	3	2	1	0
Help from faculty in seeing the value of their subject to you	_____	_____	4	3	2	1	0
Tutoring or other help in improving learning habits, writing, etc..	_____	_____	4	3	2	1	0
Help with financial problems: financial aid, job finding, etc.	_____	_____	4	3	2	1	0
Counseling concerning who you are and what you want — academically and personally	_____	_____	4	3	2	1	0

PLEASE USE SPACE BELOW AND ON REVERSE SIDE FOR ANY ADDITIONAL
COMMENTS

McKENDREE COLLEGE

The McKendree College Survey

Please Note

In this questionnaire you are asked what you are doing now, and what kinds of experiences you had at McKendree. This survey depends upon the sincerity and frankness with which you answer the questions. Your cooperation, the vital factor in the success of the study, is greatly appreciated.

Start Here

1. What are you doing at the present time? (Please be specific. For example: "I am a full time student at McKendree College majoring in elementary education," or "I am married and working while my husband attends University of Illinois," etc.)

_____

_____

_____

2. If you are no longer at McKendree College please give your reason or reasons for leaving. (For example: "I graduated from McKendree," "I couldn't find other students who shared my interests so I enrolled at Illinois State University after my freshman year," or "My grades were disappointing so I transferred to Eastern Illinois University," etc.)

_____

_____

_____

_____

3. Below is a list of some experiences and situations which students have sometimes named as having troubled them during their years at McKendree College. For each situation consider *how much of a problem* it was or has been for YOU at *McKendree*. Please circle ONE alternative for EACH statement.

Problems	Extremely important problem for me	Very important problem for me	Fairly important problem for me	Not Too important problem for me	Not At All important problem for me
A difficulty developing proper study habits— utilizing my time	4	3	2	1	0
A difficulty in meeting the academic standards of the College	4	3	2	1	0
The failure of the course- work to challenge me intellectually	4	3	2	1	0

Problems	Extremely important problem for me	Very important problem for me	Fairly important problem for me	Not Too important problem for me	Not At All important problem for me
An inability to enroll in courses leading to my career objective which is_____	4	3	2	1	0
A doubt about the value of obtaining a college degree	4	3	2	1	0
Uncertainty about my career objective—what I want to do in life	4	3	2	1	0
An atmosphere in the residence halls which is not conducive to: (a) a pleasant social life	4	3	2	1	0
(b) an environment for study	4	3	2	1	0
A feeling that I was not getting proper student services (counseling, etc.)	4	3	2	1	0
A difficulty in relating to other students	4	3	2	1	0
A problem in financing my education	4	3	2	1	0
A feeling of being isolated because of the (a) size of the College	4	3	2	1	0
(b) size of the town	4	3	2	1	0
(c)_____	4	3	2	1	0
A disappointment in: (a) academic advising	4	3	2	1	0
(b) personal advising	4	3	2	1	0
A feeling of not being involved in the decision-making process	4	3	2	1	0

The foregoing list is by no means intended to exhaust the set of situations encountered by students. Therefore you are invited and encouraged to elaborate some concerns which stand out as important in your experience at McKendree College. (Use extra sheets if necessary.)

_____

_____

_____

4. Until this point the questions have been about situations which have been a concern to you. Now we wish your personal *evaluation* of the following services or facilities at McKendree College:

	I have no basis on which to make a judgment	Fully adequate– nothing more needed	Generally adequate– satisfactory OK	Clearly inadequate– much more needs to be done
Advising and counseling				
Personal	3	2	1	0
Academic	3	2	1	0
Career	3	2	1	0
Library services	3	2	1	0
Placement services	3	2	1	0
Health services	3	2	1	0
Book store services	3	2	1	0
Food services	3	2	1	0
Security services	3	2	1	0
Admissions Program	3	2	1	0
College publications (Catalog, etc.)	3	2	1	0
Religious life activities	3	2	1	0
Services of the campus center (Deneen)	3	2	1	0
Student activities— Concerts, lectures, etc.	3	2	1	0
Student newspaper	3	2	1	0
Intramural program	3	2	1	0
Intercollegiate athletic program	3	2	1	0
Process of admissions	3	2	1	0
Process of applying for financial aids	3	2	1	0

Process of registration	3	2	1	0
Process of student billing	3	2	1	0
Process of orientation and testing	3	2	1	0
Community-college relations	3	2	1	0
Physical facilities				
Classrooms	3	2	1	0
Chapel	3	2	1	0
Library	3	2	1	0
Bookstore	3	2	1	0
Dining Hall	3	2	1	0
Residence Hall	3	2	1	0
Student Union	3	2	1	0
Gymnasium	3	2	1	0
Parking	3	2	1	0

So far your advice has been on areas where the College can provide additional help and service. Now we would appreciate it if you will mention the aspects of our program which you feel are strong, that is, they have been particularly satisfying to you.

_____
_____
_____
_____
_____
_____
_____
_____
_____
_____
_____

Again your time is greatly appreciated. Thank You

_____

Name (optional)

Please return questionnaire to

Director of Institutional Research
McKendree College
Lebanon, Ill. 62254

COLLEGE OF SAINT BENEDICT   Name _____

                                  Address _____

                                  _____

Questionnaire on Freshman Students of 1973–74 Who Left the College
During or at the End of That Academic Year

A. Check the column which seems to complete the statement best.

	Very Satis-factory	Satis-factory	Average	Unsatis-factory	Very unsatis-factory
1. The orientation programs I participated in at CSB were					
2. The living conditions were					
3. The meal service I received was					
4. My relationship with other CSB students was					
5. I thought the concern and help I received from faculty and administration was					
6. The relationship I had with my faculty adviser was					
7. The counseling services I received were					
8. I thought most of my classes, in terms of interest, content, and teaching methods were					
9. I thought the college requirements were					
10. The quality of the department in which I chose to major was					
11. My financial aid was					

B. Please rank in order of importance the four reasons why you left the College of Saint Benedict. (Use *1* for strongest reason, *2* for less strong, etc.)

_____ The College did not offer the course of study that interested me. Which course of study?

_____ The costs were too high.

_____ I decided college wasn't for me. (Please explain on reverse side.)

_____ I transferred to another college with a stronger department in my area of interest.

_____ I wanted to marry.

_____ I wanted a large college in a city.

_____ There wasn't enough social life.

_____ I couldn't get along with my roommate or other students.

_____ I wasn't academically challenged.

_____ Financial aid wasn't sufficient.

_____ I didn't want to go to SJU for courses.

_____ CSB was too far from home.

_____ CSB was too close to home.

_____ I was bored.

_____ The College was not what I expected it to be.

C. If you have comments that will help us with our survey, please write below.

Please return this form to Sister Firmin Escher, College of Saint Benedict, Saint Joseph, Minnesota 56374 by November 5, 1974.

So that the College has more information about you and what you are doing, would you please help us by filling out this information and returning it with your questionnaire. Thank you.

Your present address: _____

_____

_____

If you are in school, what is the college or institution you are attending?

_____

What course of study are you taking? _____

If you are not in school but employed, what is your employment?

_____

Any other comments.

Thank you.

APPENDIX G   MISCELLANEOUS QUESTIONS USEFUL IN STUDIES OF STUDENT PERFORMANCE AND SATISFACTION *

First, some Questions on Your Feelings About College and Michigan

- Have any of your relatives attended the University of Michigan, now or previously? (Check as many of the following as apply)

    _____ Father
    _____ Mother
    _____ Brother
    _____ Sister
    _____ Other relatives
    _____ No relatives have attended Michigan.

- Will all your brothers and sisters probably attend college, or will some of them settle down without going to college? (Check one)

    _____ Probably all will go (or all have been)
    _____ Probably one or more will not go
    _____ I have no brothers or sisters

- About how much will the sources below be contributing to the costs of your education (including living expenses) this year? (Check one for *each* source.)

*Adapted from *Characteristics of Entering Freshmen Related to Attrition in the Literary College of a Large State University,* by Gerald Gurin, Theodore Newcomb and Robert Cope. Final Research Report to the U.S. Department of Health, Education, and Welfare: Office of Education, January 1968.

	All or nearly all	More than half	About half	Less than half	None
Parents, wife, or husband	___	___	___	___	___
Own part-time and summer work	___	___	___	___	___
Scholarship	___	___	___	___	___
Other (Please specify)					
_____	___	___	___	___	___

● People have different ideas about *what they look forward to in college,* or *what they hope to achieve there.* Please indicate how important *each* of the following ideas is to you, according to this scheme:

Write in + + if the idea is of great importance
Write in + if the idea is of moderate importance
Write in 0 if the idea is of little or no importance

_____ Getting prepared for marriage and family life
_____ Thinking through what kind of occupation and career I want, and developing some of the necessary skills
_____ Having fun; enjoying the last period before assuming adult responsibilities
_____ Exploring new ideas—the excitement of learning
_____ Establishing meaningful friendships
_____ Finding myself; discovering what kind of person I really want to be
_____ Opportunities to think through what I really believe, what values are important to me
_____ Developing a deep, perhaps professional grasp of a specific field of study

Please read carefully

● Now, go back and look at *those that you rated + +.* Put a "1" in front of the one that is *most important* to you, and a "2" in front of the one that is *second most important.*

● What were your *first three* choices for college, in order of your preference?

1st choice _____

2nd choice _____

3rd choice _____

● How sure are you that you made the right choice in coming to Michigan? (Check one)

_____ Very sure

_____ Fairly sure

_____ Not at all sure

● What part would you say that your parents played in your decision to come to Michigan? (Check one statement for father and one for mother)

	Mother	Father
It's largely at his (her) insistence that I am here	_____	_____
Played a critical role in the decision— really helped me think it through	_____	_____
Played a supportive, encouraging role— was interested, but I really thought it through myself	_____	_____
Had very little to do with it	_____	_____
Was really against my decision	_____	_____
Parent deceased	_____	_____

● How important is it to you to graduate from college? (Check one)

_____ Extremely important

_____ Fairly important

_____ Not very important

● Below are some reasons which may be important in deciding which college or university to go to. Go through the list *quickly* and check *each one* that was *important* to you *in selecting Michigan.*

_____ Very good college for training in my field

_____ Intellectual reputation of Michigan

_____ Good athletic program		_____	Rewarding social life on campus
_____ High academic standing			
_____ Close to home		_____	Very good college for my intellectual development
_____ Didn't want to be too close to home		_____	Family tradition
_____ Low-cost college, chance to work		_____	Influence or wishes of father
_____ Coeducational college		_____	Influence or wishes of high school teacher
_____ Receipt of a scholarship		_____	Couldn't go to the college of my real choice
_____ Influence or wishes of mother		_____	Wanted to go to a different place than where my friends were going
_____ My friends are going here			
_____ Wanted to go to a different place than where others in my family had gone		_____	My sister (brother) is already going to Michigan

Please read carefully

• Now go back over *all the items that you have checked*, and rank the *three* of them that were the most important in your decision to come here. Put a "1" before the one of *greatest importance*, a "2" before the *next most important*, and a "3" before the one *third in importance*.

Now, Some Questions on Your Plans and Expectations for College

• Do you have a major or an academic field of interest in mind now?

     _____ Yes (Answer Question 10a)
     _____ No (Answer Question 10b)

10a. (if yes) What is it? _____
How certain are you that you will major in this field of interest? (Check one)
     _____ Very certain
     _____ Fairly certain
     _____ Not too certain

10b. (if no) What majors are you considering?
_____

● How do you feel you will handle the work at Michigan? (Check one)

    _____ I feel entirely confident that I can handle my work here at Michigan

    _____ Generally speaking, I should be able to do the work, but I may have trouble here and there

    _____ I expect some trouble in most of my courses but I should manage to get by

    _____ I think I may have a great deal of difficulty

● Below are listed six important areas, or interests, in life. People differ in the emphasis or degree of importance that they attribute to each of these interests.

Please rank the six interests in terms of their IMPORTANCE TO YOU. Insert "1" before the area of greatest importance, "2" before the next most important to you, and so on down to "6" representing the least important to you.

Please note. Your response should be made to the *complete statement* about each of the interests, and not just to the first word, which is only a convenient label; what that word means to you may not at all correspond to the statement following.

    _____ *Theoretical:* empirical, critical, or rational matters— observing and reasoning, ordering and systematizing, discovering truths.

    _____ *Economic:* that which is useful and practical, especially the practical affairs of the business world; preference for judging things by their tangible utility.

    _____ *Aesthetic:* beauty, form, and harmony for its own sake; an artistic interpretation of life.

    _____ *Social:* human relationships and love; interest in human beings for their own sake.

    _____ *Political:* power and influence; leadership and competition

    _____ *Religious:* religious experience as providing satisfaction and meaning; interest in relating oneself to the unity of the universe as a whole

Some Background Information

- How old are you?

_____ (and) _____
years   months

- Check one of the following places which best describes the place *where you lived most of your life.*

_____ On a farm or in a village (2500 population or less)
_____ In a town (2500 to 9999)
_____ In a small city (10,000 to 49,999)
_____ In a medium city (50,000 to 200,000)
_____ In a metropolitan city (200,000 or more)
_____ In a suburb of a metropolitan city close to and almost part of the city.

- Where is your *home* address *now?* (Please do not answer in terms of school residence)

_____   _____   _____
         (city)   (state)   (country)

- What is your marital status?

_____ Single, not going steady
_____ Single, going steady
_____ Single, engaged
_____ Married
_____ Widowed, divorced, separated

- How often do your parents attend religious services? (Check for each parent)

Father   Mother

_____ _____ Once a week or more
_____ _____ Two or three times a month
_____ _____ Once a month
_____ _____ A few times a year
_____ _____ Rarely over the years
_____ _____ Never
_____ _____ Parent deceased

- What is your religious preference?

_____	Protestant (Please specify denomination) _____
_____	Catholic
_____	Jewish
_____	Other (Please specify) _____
_____	None

- How often do you attend religious services? (Check one)

_____	Once a week or more
_____	Two or three times a month
_____	Once a month
_____	A few times a year
_____	Rarely over the years
_____	Never

- Do you think of yourself as more religious, about as religious, or less religious than your parents? (Check one for each parent)

	Father	Mother
I am more religious than	_____	_____
I am about as religious as	_____	_____
I am less religious than	_____	_____
Parent deceased	_____	_____

- How far did your parents go in school? (Check on for each parent)

Father	Mother	
_____	_____	Less than high school
_____	_____	Some high school (9–11 years)
_____	_____	Completed high school (12 years)
_____	_____	Some college
_____	_____	Completed college
_____	_____	Advanced or professional degree

- What is your father's occupation (or, if he is retired or deceased, what was it before)? Kindly give a full answer, such as "high school chemistry teacher," "welder in an aircraft factory," "president of a small automobile agency," "manager of a large department store."

_____
_____
_____
_____

- Are you (Check one)

  _____ an only child
  _____ the oldest child
  _____ the youngest child
  _____ none of these

- How many brothers do you have? _____

- How many sisters do you have? _____

- About how much total income do your parents earn yearly at the present time? (Check on)

  _____ Less than $3999
  _____ $4000 to $7499
  _____ $7500 to $9999
  _____ $10,000 to $14,999
  _____ $15,000 to $19,999
  _____ $20,000 and over

How certain are you about his income? (Check one)

  _____ I am quite certain about it
  _____ I know it approximately
  _____ I'm mostly guessing

High School Background

- About how many students were there in your high school *graduating class?* (Check one)

_____ 49 or less

_____ 50–99

_____ 100–149

_____ 150–199

_____ 200–299

_____ 300–399

_____ 400–499

_____ 500–599

_____ 600 and more

- To the best of your knowledge, what was your academic rank in your high school graduating class? (Check one)

_____ Top 2%

_____ Top 10%

_____ Top 25%

_____ Top 50%

_____ Below top 50%

- Check the one of the following which is closest to the grade average you expect to have at the end of this year.

A+ A A–   B+ B B–   C+ C C–   D+ D D–   F
— — —   — — —   — — —   — — —   —

- Do you expect to continue your education in a graduate or professional school after completing your undergraduate degree? (Check one)

_____ Definitely yes

_____ Probably yes

_____ Probably not

_____ Definitely not

_____ Don't know

If you check "definitely" or "probably " yes, in what field of study?

_____

- How active do you think you will be in extracurricular activities on campus? (Check one)

_____ Extremely active
_____ Quite active
_____ Moderately active
_____ Not very active
_____ Don't know

If you feel that you will become involved in extracurricular activities, which do you think you will probably become most involved in?

_____

_____

_____

Now a Few Questions About Living Arrangements.

- First, if you had a choice, would you prefer to live alone or to have a roommate? (Check one)

    _____ Much prefer to live alone
    _____ Somewhat prefer to live alone
    _____ Somewhat prefer to have a roommate
    _____ Much prefer to have a roommate

- If you were to have a roommate, would you prefer someone you knew before you came to the University or would you prefer someone you didn't know before? (Check one)

    _____ Much prefer someone I knew before
    _____ Somewhat prefer someone I knew before
    _____ Somewhat prefer someone I did not know before
    _____ Much prefer someone I did not know before

- Would you like to affiliate with a fraternity or sorority? (check one)

    _____ Yes
    _____ No
    _____ Uncertain

Some Questions On Your Experiences Before Coming to College

- We're interested in the things students do in the way of self-expression—things they do outside of class, for their own interests. Thinking over the past four years, have you done any of the following? (Check all that you have done during your high school years and *double-check* any that you have *particularly enjoyed*.)

_____ Writing poetry
_____ Playing in jazz combo
_____ Playing in school band, orchestra
_____ Acting in plays
_____ Composing music
_____ Writing a play
_____ Arranging orchestrated music
_____ Writing a short story or a novel
_____ Taking part in debates, forensics
_____ Writing feature articles, essays
_____ Doing painting, drawing, or sculpture
_____ Building a car out of old parts
_____ Fixing things (appliances, furniture)
_____ Designing furniture, buildings
_____ Directing a play
_____ Decorating my room, designing clothes
_____ Working on an independent scientific project
_____ Finding mathematical solutions for difficult problems
_____ Inventing something

• Are there any things which were of very special interest to you during your high school years—*we mean things that had very special meaning to you, something beyond the usual.* For example, has there ever been any subject matter, project, topic that you've been really involved in (enough to explore on your own or work on beyond the requirements of a course), or any activity (either school-connected or something unrelated to high school) that you've put a great deal of yourself into, that has had a special meaning to you? (Don't feel forced to answer yes.)

_____ Yes   _____ No, not really

If Yes, what was it?

_____

_____

_____

APPENDIX H OMNIBUS PERSONALITY INVENTORY: DEFINITIONS OF SELECTED SCALES WITH REPRESENTATIVE ITEMS[1]

SCALES

Religious Liberalism (RL)—measures how liberal a person is in his ideological commitments, high scores being skeptical of conventional, orthodox religious beliefs and practices.

Estheticism (ES)—measures diverse interest in artistic matters and activities including literature, dramatics, painting, music, and sculpture. High scores have greater interests in these areas.

Complexity (CO)—measures how much a person tends to be comfortable with ambiguity, uncertainty, and novelty. High scorers may prefer complexity to simplicity and tend to need diversity and avoid excessive structure.

Impulse Expression (IE)—measures readiness to express feeling and seek gratification in conscious thought or action. Low scorers may tend to be rigid and constrained.

Social Maturity (SM)—high scorers are *not* authoritarian; they tend to be flexible, tolerant, and realistic in their thinking. High scorers are also frequently interested in intellectual and esthetic pursuits.

Theoretical Orientation (TO)—measures interest in science and in scientific method in thinking. High scorers are generally logical, rational, and critical in their approach to problems.

Thinking Introversion (TI)—measures liking for reflective thought, particularly of an abstract nature. High scorers have a greater preference for reflective thought.

REPRESENTATIVE ITEMS

Religious Liberalism (RL)
    (a) I believe in a real life hereafter. (F)

[1]From the 1962 OPI Manual, pp. 4–6.

(b) In matters of religion it really does not matter what one be-
ieves. (T)

Estheticism (ES)
(a) I enjoy listening to poetry. (T)
(b) I like dramatics. (T)

Complexity (CO)
(a) I dislike following a set schedule. (T)
(b) For most questions there is just one right answer, once a person
is able to get all the facts. (F)

Impulse Expression (IE)
(a) I find that a well-ordered mode of life with regular hours is not
congenial to my temperament. (T)
(b) When I get bored I like to stir up some excitement. (T) *Social
Maturity* (SM)
(a) I prefer people who are never profane. (F)
(b) Unquestioning obedience is not a virtue. (T)

Theoretical Orientation (TO)
(a) I like to discuss philosophical problems. (T)
(b) My free time is usually filled up by social demands. (F)

Thinking Introversion (TI)
(a) I like to read serious, philosophical poetry. (T)
(b) I study and analyze my own motives and reactions. (T)

AUTHOR INDEX

SUBJECT INDEX